Artistic Woodturning

Artistic Woodturning

Dale L. Nish

Brigham Young University Press

Cover photo by Beth Erickson.

Library of Congress Cataloging in Publication Data

Nish, Dale L   1932–
  Artistic woodturning.

  Includes index.
  1. Turning. I. Title.
TT201.N55   684'.083   80-21302
ISBN 0-8425-1842-8
ISBN 0-8425-1826-6 (pbk.)

Brigham Young University Press, Provo, Utah
© 1980 Brigham Young University Press. All rights reserved
Printed in the United States of America
9/80   2.5Mc   5Mp   46777

Contents

Foreword

After studying his first book, *Creative Woodturning,* I knew I had to get Dale Nish to instruct at the Woodturning Symposium, in Philadelphia, and fast! And he proved himself one of the best instructors we have had at any symposium. Dale's first book is one of the finest publications of its type. And this second book, *Artistic Woodturning,* has the same quality and appeal. It can be used both as a resource guide to new and innovative techniques and approaches to the lathe and as a shop manual for jigs, turning techniques, and design and project ideas.

This is an excellent guide for the woodturner— beginner and expert. Dale's ability to explain woodturning gives the reader a clear, concise picture of approaches to the art of woodturning. His writing style allows us to understand the material and then to try the various techniques in our own shops. *Artistic Woodturning* gives us an opportunity to try the old and the new techniques and approaches to the lathe. This book helps us apply technique, style, and design.

My involvement with the Woodturning Symposium brings me in contact with many woodturners and their techniques and approaches to the lathe. With the growing variety of approaches to the lathe, I am glad that Dale Nish has taken the time to present this information in such a text. In the ''Gallery of Craftsmen,'' Dale features the work of many of the finest woodturners in America—including some of the less well known woodturners who offer some very innovative styles and techniques.

A major portion of this book is devoted to projects. Ranging from the simple to the provocative, these projects can help the woodturner expand his level of excellence in woodturning. If you are a serious woodturner, this book, like Dale's first, belongs in your shop!

Albert Le Coff
Woodturning Symposium
Philadelphia, PA

Plate. Box elder. Dale L. Nish.

Nature's Designs

The other day some students and I were working a number of planks that had been cut several years ago. Some of the planks were checked, warped, and dirt covered, so we severely end-trimmed and ripped them, creating a lot of firewood. The fellows picked up an ash plank that had bark on both edges but obviously was badly infested with wood borers and powder-post beetles. Asked, "What good is this?" I replied without thinking, "Cut it up for firewood." But when noon arrived and the others had stopped for lunch, I took another look at the rejected ash pieces and wondered about their possibilities. Carefully examining a piece, I became intrigued with the pattern left by the borers and beetles. Needless to say, when the fellows returned from lunch, I was busily completing a "wormwood" turning.

From a rejected piece of wood emerged a tribute to the possibilities of nature's designs. The borers had penetrated one side of the plank. The sapwood was infested with them, their random design gradually disappearing near the heartwood. The turning emphasized the interior space created by the borers' bold design. The other side of the piece was infested with the powder-post beetle. Theirs was an intricate, lacy piece of work, a dainty, fragile construction by minute creatures involved in the business of living.

To fully appreciate nature's designs, we need to change our thinking about wood. Our thinking must accommodate change; configurations and malformations need not be defects. We should accept them for what they are—design opportunities and possibilities.

Too often we are restricted and limited by "defects" in the wood. But "defective" according to whom? To some of us the perfect tree would be straight, square, and free from limbs and branches. What a forest that would make!

George Nakashima, a skilled woodworker from Bucks County, Pennsylvania, specializes in working with wood from aged trees, usually past their prime and often of little interest to the commercial lumberman. Nakashima's catalog states, "Lumber with the most interest sometimes poses the most difficult problems, and so often the best figuring is accompanied by knots, areas of worm holes, deep openings, cracks, checks and other so-called defects. . . . Just short of being worthless, a board often has the most potential and can be almost human in that respect."

We should capitalize on any freedom from the restrictions on sawing and grading normally imposed by market expectations. The interesting, one-of-a-kind piece of wood seldom reaches the traditional market. It is rejected because of its "defects."

We need to emphasize the natural features of the wood—knots, color changes caused by minerals or fungus, holes created by insects and other animals, cracks or checks, and other natural conditions. We need to learn to *see* what we are looking at, and to capitalize on the nature of the material. Wood is an organic material. Fungus will penetrate it, leaving a magic landscape ready for a turner to produce a three-dimensional canvas for displaying nature's painting. Wood is essential in the life cycle of certain insects. Using wood with these natural features is no cause for apology. Capitalize on the possibilities; you'll discover new, unexpected vistas. Like people, trees grow old. And as in people, aging in trees produces unique qualities and possibilities. Observe the differences and treasure them. Most people are *not* looking for the exceptional piece of wood; they want the average piece, and that is what is on the market. But some of us are looking for that unique piece. The lumberyard is not the place to look, though; chances are much better in your neighbor's firewood pile.

Trees have limbs and branches. And branches produce knots, which are generally thought of as defects. But are they? The swirls, the figure variations around knots, the knots themselves can be integrated into the design as accents or points of interest.

Man's activities cause foreign materials to penetrate the tree and leave their mark. A sugar maple may have the marks of a drill, and the sap may have carried stains some distance through the wood. What a display feature! A farmer may fasten a fence to a tree, and kids may drive nails into the trunk or build houses in the branches. The resulting metal will cause streaks in the wood. Use them to your advantage. A dull saw chain or bandsaw blade is a small price to pay for the opportunity to display stories told by the wood itself.

Bowls, plates, and containers. Primarily American
Hardwoods. Turned green, seasoned, and finished.
Dale L. Nish.

Harvesting Green Wood*

In the several years I have been working with green wood, the satisfaction of finding the wood has been almost as fulfilling as actually working it. Sometimes, as in life generally, the anticipation is the best part. Once while deer hunting, I found a large, soft maple burl growing at the base of a small tree. The burl encircled the tree, rising to a height of perhaps thirty inches with a diameter of more than forty-eight inches. Over several years I envisioned the turnings that could be obtained from a burl of such beauty and size. Then, at long last, I received permission to cut it off. Carrying the necessary tools and equipment (a major undertaking, as the burl was far off the road), a friend and I arrived at the tree and began to saw. The chain was sharp, and the chips flew. Then, suddenly, the bar fell into the burl! It was completely hollow. The only sound wood was a two- to three-inch shell. The burl was of no value at all for turning. Maybe next time.

The sources of wood for turning or carving are limited only by your patience and perseverence. The best wood cannot be purchased from a lumberyard or hardwood dealer, and even if the desired species is available, you will still be limited by the available sizes. Most of us live where species growing locally far exceed species available commercially, but if you want to work local wood, you must cut your own.

Wood is everywhere. Robert L. Butler, in his book *Wood for Wood Carvers and Craftsmen* (Cranbury, N.J.: A.S. Barnes Co., 1975), has a chapter aptly titled "Wood Is Where You Find It." In Utah, which is not noted for its forests, I have harvested locally grown oak, ash, maple, black locust, honey locust, mulberry, English and black walnut, American and Siberian elm, ailanthus, catalpa, cottonwood, poplar, box elder, aspen, chestnut, sycamore, apple, pear, cherry, plum, peach, apricot, and more. Wood is everywhere. I have found it in firewood stacks, trees bulldozed to clear building sites, limbs left from logging operations, windfalls after a storm, and orchards being uprooted. Other good sources of turning and carving wood are tree-removal companies, city shade-tree departments, local sawmills, landfill or dump areas, and friends and neighbors who know you are a wood nut and inform you when they see trees being cleared. Local sawmills frequently have short or crooked logs that have been discarded as uneconomical for processing into lumber. These logs are either inexpensive or free. Show your appreciation with a gift of a turning or two, and see how your supply increases.

A minimum of equipment is required for cutting your own wood. A chain saw is a necessity, and you will also need a maul, splitting wedges, and a peavey (if the trees are large). A pickup or trailer is handy, but you will be surprised how much wood you can haul in the trunk of your car.

The chain saw must be sharp and in good condition. I use a chain saw with a sixteen-inch bar for most of my cutting, but I have a saw with a thirty-inch bar for larger pieces. In Utah it is uncommon for a tree to be more than thirty inches in diameter.

The chain must be sharpened according to manufacturer's specifications—teeth even in length and equally sharp, or the saw will lead toward the sharp side of the bar. If the saw has an automatic oiler, check to be sure it works. Usually the oil reservoir must be filled each time you fill the saw with gas. Manual oilers must be used frequently, as improper oiling or insufficient oil will raise havoc with the bar and chain. Always use ear protection: Many saws can cause permanent ear damage after a short time of continuous use.

---

*Adapted from the author's article, by the same title, published in *Fine Woodworking* May/June 1979, pp. 48–51.

Cutting the Wood

1.   If the tree is standing, it should be felled so as to prevent damage to the tree, other trees, buildings, and equipment. As the picture indicates, this tree was felled incorrectly, and a good part of the wood was damaged.

2.   To prevent damage to the tree, the proper steps should be used. Make the undercut about a third of the way into the trunk on the side toward which the tree is leaning. This is done by making a horizontal cut into the tree (1), coming up at an angle to make the undercut (2), and removing the wedge of wood. The third cut (3) is made an inch or two above the first cut. It should extend about a third of the distance into the trunk. Next, remove the chain saw and drive a wooden wedge into the cut. Usually the tree will fall. If it does not, reinsert the chain saw (the wedge will permit you to do so) and deepen the cut.

For further information on felling a tree, consult a chain-saw manual or Robert L. Butler's book, *Wood for Wood Carvers and Craftsmen.*

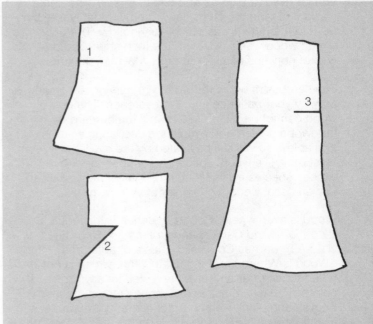

3.   The first step in working a bolt (log section) is cutting off its ends to remove the end checks. If you are concerned about nails or dirt in the bark or wood, remove the bark with an ax. However, this isn't always necessary. I usually leave the bark on the log until I am ready to work it. The bark helps keep the log from drying out and checking. But it also encourages grubs and beetles that can ruin the log, or at least the sapwood. If you remove the bark, cover the log with plastic to prevent drying and checking.

4. After the end checks are removed, measure the useful diameter of the log and cut lengths equal to, or in multiples of, that diameter.

5. The useful diameter will change from one log section to the next, so adjust your measurements accordingly. Don't cut short lengths until you are ready to work them; they check quickly, and the bolt may be ruined.

6. When laying out the cutting marks, you will want to remove, or at least allow for, defects such as this dead branch. The area will be penetrated with dead or decaying wood and will show color and grain changes. What you do will depend on how you feel about using this type of material.

7. This type of growth, sometimes called a "cat's eye," is created when a limb is cut off and the wound covered with bark. The area may be sound, but more likely it will have some decay. Certainly there will be change in color and grain pattern. Again, what you do is a matter of personal preference, but often the possibilities inherent in a piece such as this will produce a unique turning.

8. When working a cylindrical bolt (log section), I stand it on wood blocks or slabs. Be sure the bolt is in stable position for sawing. The bolt may be laid out in various ways, depending on defects, pith position, and the intended final use for the bolt.

Large checks are sometimes good places to make the cuts. Try to cut with the sawbar held at an angle of about 45 degrees, entering the bolt at the outer edge. Cutting parallel to the end of the log is inefficient because you are cutting end grain, and cutting parallel to the length of the bolt produces long shavings that cannot clear the chain, making it bind and overheat. Short bolts can be cut standing on end; long bolts must be laid down for sawing. Both types of bolt must be secure and must be raised sufficient to allow the chain to cut without contacting dirt or rocks.

9. One thing is constant: The pith should be removed from the flitches, because the pith is almost certain to cause radial checking. The alternative is to be prepared to use the polyethylene glycol (PEG 1000) treatment.

To cut a bolt, outline the cuts on the end of the bolt. Then make cuts (1,2) parallel to the top and bottom of each flitch. These cuts should remove most of the bark. Don't cut too deeply; the sapwood can be used to add interest and color to the turning. (Fruitwoods, however, are an exception: Their sapwood is almost impossible to season without checking and should be removed.)

10. The next step is to make the primary cut (1), which usually will halve the bolt. The following cuts (2) remove the pith. Any remaining bark should be removed with an ax.

Cutting for figure. Most of the pretty figured wood in a tree will occur in the area below the major fork ("crotch figure"), in the stump area ("stump figure"), or in the occasional burl on the trunk or around the base of the tree. Crotch figure, the most beautiful, is seldom found commercially because it is trimmed off at the mill, or is so thin or short that it has little value. Some of the finest crotch figures I have found came from local cottonwood trees on their way to the dump. Cottonwood trees, at least in Utah, have little commercial value and are seldom used even for firewood. Other species with beautiful crotch wood are honey locust, black walnut, elm, ash, catalpa, aspen, cherry, and apricot.

Some trees are consistent winners in producing fine crotch figure, and walnut is one of the most consistent.

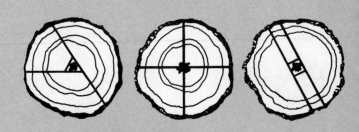

Lay the bolt out according to how many bowls will fit, pith and any defects.

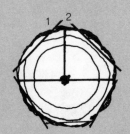

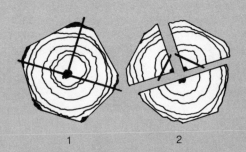

Crotch Wood

11.   If I have a complete tree, I try to work the major crotch first. If I am interested in wood for gun stocks, my first two cuts, after removing the small branches and limbs, are about two feet above the fork of the tree. If I am planning to use the wood for turning, I cut just above the junction of the major limbs. These cuts sever the two major limbs from the trunk.

The next cut is made two to three feet below the fork.

Before making this cut, be sure to support the underside of the trunk with wooden blocks or wedges to prevent the trunk from settling and binding the saw blade.

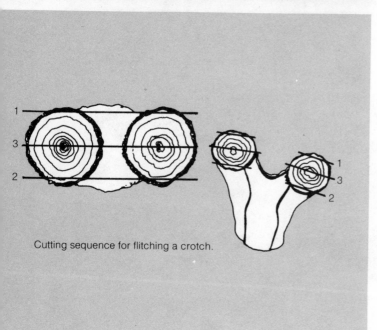

Cutting sequence for flitching a crotch.

12.   After cutting the fork from the tree, examine the ends for decay, splitting, insect activity, and other deterioration. Using a lumber crayon, mark the pith on the ends of the fork. If the fork is sound, transfer the crayon marks to the sides of the fork. Use a straightedge to connect the marks from top to bottom. These lines will be the cut lines when the fork is split.

Using the center line as a guide, saw a slab from both sides of the fork, trying to keep the cut parallel to the center line. The slab cuts should remove part of the sapwood and bark, but they should not be so deep that they remove wood that could be used during turning. Watch for nails or other metal, and pull or chop them out of the wood. Expect to hit a few nails if the trees come from yards or fence lines. Sharpening a chain is a small price to pay for a quality piece of wood, and in my experience a nail or piece of wire does much less damage to the chain than does a small rock or pocket of sandy dirt.

After the slab cuts are complete, saw down the center line. Do not try to saw straight across, parallel to the ends of the forks. Rather, angle the cut at about 45 degrees to the end-grain surface. This allows the chain to cut more efficiently. Too little angle and the wood being cut out by the chain will resemble sawdust; too much angle and the result is long slivers or shavings that clog the chain drive. Experience will show you the best cutting angle. If the fork is large, you may have to cut from both sides until you reach the main trunk below the fork. Start the cuts carefully, and be sure they line up and will meet at the junction of the fork. A cut running off to one side will require extra work and could ruin a piece of wood of exceptional beauty and value. A perfect cut would be right down the pith of the tree, leaving part of the pith in each piece. This would produce two true flat slabs and minimal waste. It is always exciting to make this cut and watch the fork separate. I can hardly wait to see what is revealed. It is better than Christmas, and it happens every time I work a piece of wood.

13. Some trees, such as black walnut, will have crotch figures wherever a branch attaches to the trunk or larger branch. Other trees may not have true crotch figure, but you can always find beautiful figure in that area. Crotch figure of small trees is thin, often only an inch or two deep. To preserve it, shallow trays or plates must be turned with the figure at the bottom, so that one can turn down to it and reveal it. Otherwise, the turner will go through the figured area into the plain wood, leaving the figure visible only at the edges.

Stumpwood

14. Stumpwood is the part of the tree that starts to flare at the base of the trunk and continues into the ground. Usually a tree is cut off a foot or two above the ground, leaving the stump intact. Sawing off the stump close to the ground often yields an excellent piece of wood. Sometimes the stump may be dug out

completely. Then the roots are cut off and the remaining stumpwood cut up.

Because stump figure goes all the way through the blocks, stumpwood usually can be cut into various sizes and turned with little regard to grain direction. This wood is excellent for deep bowls of simple design.

15. Stumps often contain pockets of dirt and rocks. Make a starting cut for a wedge, and split the stump with a maul and wedges. The splitting loosens most rocks and dirt so that they can be removed easily.

Burls

16. Cut burls into their most useful sizes, disregarding grain direction. Often defects will limit the size of pieces to be turned, but if the defects are small, I often leave them in the surface of the turning.

Treating Green Flitches

Trees are designed to carry sap, and so long as a tree is alive, its cells are filled with water. However, when a tree is cut down, it begins to lose moisture. This process is called "seasoning" or "drying." As the wood loses water from the cells, it becomes lighter, harder, and stronger, and it also shrinks. Seasoning will continue until a balance is reached between the water in the wood and the moisture in the surrounding air. This balance is called "equilibrium moisture content" (EMC). Because the EMC will vary with the humidity, the final part of the seasoning should be where the wood will be used. Most often this will be in heated rooms.

1.   A bolt will begin end checking as soon as it is cut. Visible evidence will appear in as little time as a few minutes, particularly on a warm, windy day. The fresh cut ends should be coated immediately after cutting.

If the weather is hot and dry, as it often is in Utah, it may be wise to cover the bolts loosely with a plastic sheet.

2.   Green flitches should be end-coated immediately after cutting to prevent moisture loss and checking. If the flitches are to be seasoned before turning or held for a month or two before turning, I recommend applying a commercial end-coating made by Mobil Oil Co., called "Mobilcer-M." Coat the ends and about two inches in from each end, areas of high figure, knots, and (with some species) sapwood. Other end-coatings, such as hot paraffin wax, asphalt, thick oil-based paints, Vaseline, and white glue may also be used. If a flitch has been cut and left untreated for a few days and the ends are checked, make a fresh cut to remove the checks before end-coating.

3.   For temporary storage, or for storing bolts whose bark has been removed, wrap the bolts in several layers of polyethylene plastic or place them in large plastic garbage bags. The major problem of storage in plastic bags is the growth of mold, which may discolor the pieces.

4. It is very difficult to season a bolt without cutting it into flitches. Small logs and limb wood up to eight inches in diameter can often be seasoned without excessive checking, if they are kept covered and allowed to season slowly over a period of several years. I have had little success with larger pieces; they are subject to extreme radial checking. The piece in the photo was about fourteen inches in diameter and was left in a plastic bag for three years to allow it to season slowly. This photo was taken when the bag was removed. There was some checking, but I felt the piece could be cut and used for turning a bowl.

5. The above piece was cut vertically, eliminating two major radial checks, and then was placed on a band saw. This is what the first cut revealed.

A classic example of extreme checking.

6. The second cut—again extreme checking.

The third cut was similar. The piece had no value as sound, seasoned wood.

7. This piece of walnut burl, seasoned for two and a half years, showed little evidence of checking, except for some shrinkage at the surface.

8.   The end indicated some checking. (The large check was caused partially by a bark pocket.)

9.   Successive cuts showed extreme checking and honeycomb (cell collapse), making the piece worthless as a source of sound wood.

10.   It took about eight inches of stock to get down to wood that was not checked. At this point, however, the wood was wet. A moisture meter indicated a moisture content of about 28 percent at the center.

The checking would have progressed in from the opposite end about the same distance; thus, as sound wood this large block has little value.

11.   Wood should be taken care of as soon as possible after the tree has been cut. Some wood, such as this piece of walnut, will change color where it has been exposed to the sun. Also, wood borers will penetrate wood that is in contact with the ground. The bolts should be cut up, coated, and stored for future use.

Seasoning Flitches

Flitches that are to be seasoned for later use should be treated much differently than bolts. I cut flitches as long as possible, that way there will be less trimming waste when they are used. Next I weigh each piece and write its weight and the date on the flat side. Periodically thereafter I record the weight. When it stabilizes, the moisture content of the wood is in equilibrium with that of the atmosphere.

After weighing and end-coating the flitches, I stack them in an unheated shed. Sticker the flitches if they are flat and of uniform thickness, or stack them if they are of random size and thickness, to allow for good air circulation. In dry climates cover them tightly with a plastic sheet. In humid areas, you can probably leave them uncovered.

If you weigh a block of green wood on a daily basis, you will note that most of the weight loss occurs in the first few weeks. This is also the time when checking is most liable to occur. Covering the green wood with plastic gives it a chance to season slowly, without checking. If the wood has a lot of figure or is very valuable, I sometimes leave the plastic on for several months and then open the bottom of the cover to allow the outside air direct contact with the wood. Over a period of a month or two, I open the cover more and more. Eventually it is removed completely.

When the weight has been stable for several weeks, the equilibrium moisture content (EMC) has been reached. In most areas this will be between 12 and 15 percent moisture. The wood should then be brought into a heated storage area and allowed to season to between 6 and 8 percent moisture content. The time will depend on species, temperature, and thickness. Periodic weighing will indicate when the moisture in the wood has reached the EMC of the heated room. Alternatively, a good moisture meter can be used to check the wood.

Wood seasons at various rates, but you can expect at least a year per inch up to 8/4 stock, and three to four years for 12/4 or 16/4. Thick stock often takes five years or more to season, and even then is not suitable for finished turnings. Hence green turning is the best solution for working thick wood.

Top. A few of several hundred bowls the author has green-turned and seasoned.

Bottom. Bowls, green-turned from box-elder burl, ready for finishing.

Turning Partially Seasoned Wood

If it is necessary to use wood that has been seasoned in an unheated area, rough-turn the bowl to shape, leaving a wall thickness of 1/2'' to 3/4''. Remove the bowl from the lathe and allow it to sit on the bench for a week or two. Probably it will warp a little, but it should not check. If you see checks appearing, put the bowl in a plastic bag for a few days to allow the moisture content to stabilize. Then remove the bowl from the plastic bag and allow it to continue seasoning. Unless the wood has a high moisture content, one treatment in a bag is usually enough.

If during the turning process the bowl seems really damp, and you feel the moisture in the wood, complete the rough turning and treat the bowl as green wood.

After You Green-Turn. Green wood should be cut to rough shape, mounted, and turned in a manner similar to turning seasoned wood. After the bowl is green-turned to a uniform wall thickness of 3/4'' to 1'' for bowls less than eight inches in diameter, and 1'' to 1¼'' for larger bowls, I coat the surfaces, inside and out, to control checking during seasoning. Before coating the bowl, I often weigh it and write the weight and the date on the bowl.

For bowls with no problem areas, a heavy coating of paste wax usually is sufficient. Coat the end-grain carefully, forcing the wax well down into the fibers. If a bowl has high figure, knots, or sapwood, coat these areas with Mobilcer-M. Let the coating dry until it has a clear appearance, then coat the remainder of the bowl with paste wax. Place the coated bowls on the floor or on low shelves in an unheated area with little air movement. After about a month, move them to a moderately heated room. Bowls coated with paste wax will season and reach EMC in about three months. If I am in no hurry, I often dip bowls in Mobilcer-M and let them drain dry. These bowls will take six to twelve months to be ready for finish-turning.

Figure in Wood

"Figure" refers to the design or pattern on the wood surface. Grain is the primary cause of figure, but other factors, such as color, growth rate, grain type, and physical variants such as limbs, knots, burls, crotches, and stump area also affect figure. Figure is also influenced by the method of sawing, and by the prominence of medullary rays. Other configurations such as spalting, fungus penetration, colorant absorption, and the imbedding of such objects as maple taps, nails, and spikes will also affect figure.

There are many names for *figure*, and terms vary throughout the timber-producing countries. In fact the terms may not be standard within geographic areas within the same state. Some names for figure have local connotations. Other names have their basis in professional terms established by botanists. Generally, however, the terms used to describe figure are specific in their description and relate to other well-known objects or descriptions. Some common names are "crotch," "feather crotch," "plum pudding," "marble cake," "basket weave," "fiddle back," "tiger tail," "swirl," "curly," "birdseye," and "ribbon stripe." There are many others.

Grain refers to the orientation of the wood cells in relationship to the trunk. The most common pattern is straight grain, in which most of the cells are oriented parallel to the trunk. This is strong but uninteresting wood. "Irregular grain" produces many different types of figure, because the cells have many different orientations. Irregular grain is common in the areas of limbs or stumps. "Interlocked grain" is common in tropical hardwoods but not in American hardwoods. The fibers in alternate growth layers grow at right angles to each other. "Wavy grain" is created when the fiber direction shifts back and forth, producing a wavy appearance.

Cutting methods also affect figure. Most lumber is plain or flat sawed, this being the fastest and most economical method of cutting trees into lumber. Quarter-sawed lumber is less common, but some woods, such as oak and sycamore produce a beautiful, distinct figure when quarter-sawed. The figure prominently displays large flakes and stripes because the saw cuts parallel to the medullary rays. Keep in mind that plain or flat-sawed lumber will have a few boards that are in fact quarter-sawed, as they come from either side of the pith of the tree, where the saw cut is parallel to the rays.

No two pieces of wood will be exactly alike. No two pieces will have exactly the same figure. The causes of figure are many, and the possible combinations infinite. This makes wood a material unique in all the world. Appreciate the differences and your life will never again be the same.

Crotch Figure

Crotch figure, one of the most beautiful of all figures, comes in many variations. It can be found in most trees, but some such as black walnut, claro walnut, ash, elm, and maple consistently produce crotch figure of excellent quality. Black walnut will usually have crotch figure wherever a branch attaches to the trunk or larger branch. Most crotch wood comes from directly below the juncture of the primary branches and the main trunk. It has been suggested that the figure is caused by the stress and tension below the branching area, but many trees produce little or no crotch figure in that area. Usually the crotch in these trees has distinctively figured wood, but the prominent figure usually associated with crotch wood is missing.

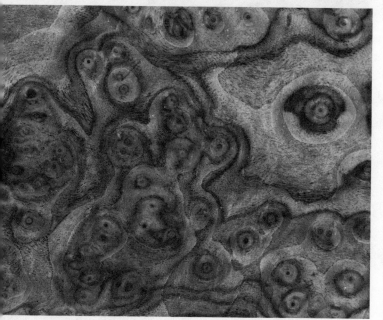

Top. Crotch figure.

Bottom. Burl.

Burls

Burls are uncommon and usually are available only as veneers, but they can be found. (However, sound burls, without bark pockets or decay, are rare.) Most often burls appear around the base of the tree, but they may appear anywhere on the main trunk. They consist of masses of dormant buds, sometimes called "eyes." Because there is no consistent alignment of wood fibers, the burl is gnarled and misshapen, producing figure of unpredictable color and pattern. And because there is no grain direction, burls are quite stable when turned green. In fact, generally they are easier to work than wood from other parts of the tree. Various theories have been advanced on the cause of burls. Speculation has centered on frost, injury, and disease produced by bacteria, fungi, or viruses, but no certain cause has been identified. However, burls are generally associated with certain species and geographic areas and with older trees. You will need to draw your own conclusion. One fact is clear: Burls offer an opportunity for turning a truly unique piece.

Stumpwood

Colors and patterns in stumpwood are innumerable. Like tree trunks, stumps contain both sapwood and heartwood, but in the stump the two woods are not evenly separated; they flow into each other. As a result, the colors are dramatic, the streaks of black and dark brown producing marblelike patterns. And because the stump is in continuous contact with the moist ground, it is subjected to mineral stains, stains from decaying surface matter, and other colorants. The irregular grain may show as quilted figure, fiddleback, ribbon, or swirl. You can expect figure equal to or better than that found in other parts of the tree, with the exception of the crotch figure. Stumpwood is usually less stable than the wood above it, however. Expect some problems with seasoning.

Graft Lines

Grafted wood, something of a rarity, always makes a conversation piece of the turning. Most grafted wood available in Utah comes from California and is English walnut grafted to claro or black walnut root stock. The English walnut produces the superior nut for the market, but the native root stock produces a more vigorous tree. The plank in the upper photo was cut at Roberts Wood Products, a Marysville, California, mill specializing in gunstock blanks. The right end of the plank is English walnut; the left, claro walnut. This is an expensive plank, but it could become a very fine shallow tray. The graft line is sound and usually is free from defect.

A bowl turned from a block of grafted wood is shown in the lower photo.

Color

Color makes some woods unique, and it is those pieces that craftsmen seek. Caused mainly by infiltrates in the cell wall, color is usually most prominent in the heartwood. Variations may be the result of soil and mineral conditions, water supply, age, growing season, and fungus activity as well as the genetic characteristics of the tree.

In Kentucky, walnut-log buyers can tell by the color, figure, and grain of a log the county and sometimes the area in the county in which the log grew.

Color and wood provide the woodturner with a rainbow assortment to choose from. Colors range from the black of the ebonies, the white of boxwood and holly, the reds of vermilion, the purple in purpleheart, and the brown of walnut, to the tans of ash and olive. And there are the mixtures found in tulipwood, rosewood, kingwood, and many others. Usually colors are at their best when the wood is fresh cut. Often they fade or darken on exposure to strong sunlight.

Magnolia. Dale L. Nish.

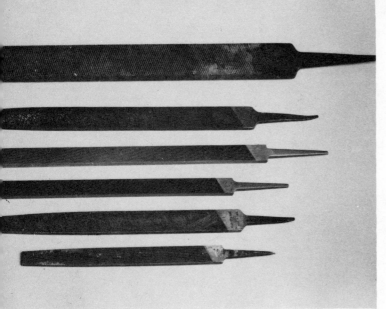

Tools and Jigs

Shop-Made Turning Tools

Conventional lathe tools purchased from traditional sources such as tool catalogs, machine dealers, or hardware stores have been and probably will remain the primary source of tools for the woodturner. However, many of us will continue to search for the exceptional tool that will "hold an edge longer," is shaped for a "special purpose," or is similar to one observed in an old woodturning book and "cannot be purchased any longer."

Scraping Tools from Files

1.   I have found files to be an excellent source of material for making scraping tools, particularly the roundnose, square-nose, and parting tools. Files can be obtained in many shapes and sizes, but many are too thin and brittle for most uses. A favorite file of mine is the Pillar file. This type is not commonly found in stores but can be purchased from industrial sources. I like it because it is thick but not too wide. It comes in various lengths, but I usually use the ten- or twelve-inch file for roundnose chisels, or for 1/2" or 5/8" square-nose chisels.

2.   Grind off the file teeth until the file is smooth on both sides.

Turn the file and grind off the teeth from the edge of the file, if necessary.

During the grinding process, keep the file cool by dipping it in water. Do not let it get hot enough to change color.

A belt grinder works best, but a grinding wheel will also do the job.

3.   Usually I cut off part of the file, reducing the length to six or eight inches, not including the tang.

Files are somewhat brittle, and a long piece may fracture more easily. Also, for better control, I prefer to work with a shorter turning tool.

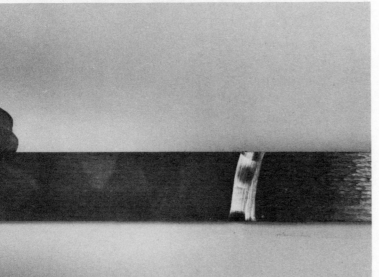

Use a grinder and make a groove 1/4 to 1/3 the thickness of the file.

4. Wrap the top part of the file in a cloth and place the tang end of the file in a vise, with the groove about 1/8" out of the vise.

Give the top part of the file a sharp blow, and the piece will snap off, leaving a relatively clean break.

Turn a handle to your specifications and set the file into the handle.

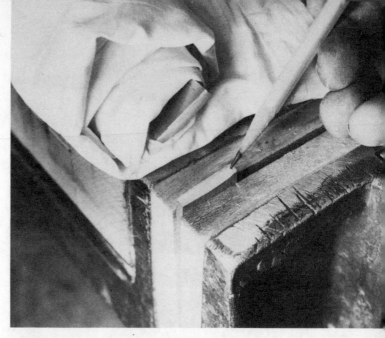

5. Grind the file to final shape, such as this roundnose.

When a scraping type tool is sharpened, do not whet or hone the edge, but use the tool just as it comes from the wheel. The wire edge left by the grinding wheel makes an excellent cutting tool. In fact, I check a scraping tool for sharpness by checking for the wire edge. If it is not on the cutting edge, I consider the tool to be "dull" and sharpen it before use. The wire edge left by a coarse wheel will not cut quite as smooth as one left by a fine wheel, so adjust your sharpening procedures accordingly.

6. A sharp roundnose with a wire edge will cut clean and sharp, producing ribbonlike shavings quickly and in large amounts.

A file made into a roundnose will hold an edge and last a long time. The hardness of the tool will be about a Rockwell "C" of 60-61. A conventional roundnose purchased from a tool company will have a hardness of approximately 55 on the Rockwell "C" scale.

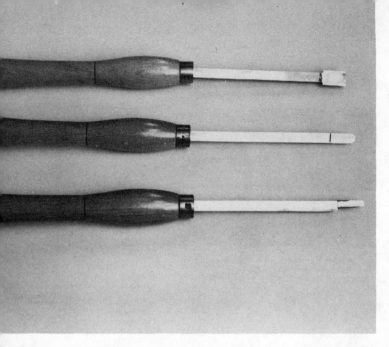

"Tipped" Tools

Various woodturners throughout the country use tools with a "tip" made from a variety of tool steels as well as carbide. One of the best methods I have encountered used pieces of planer or jointer knives to tip the tools. An eighteen-inch jointer or surfacer knife can be cut into various lengths, and will yield many tips 1⅛" to 1½" in length and whatever width required. This tip can be brazed or silver soldered to a piece of 1/2" X 1/2" mild steel square stock, and then ground to the desired shape. This type of tool will then have a very hard tip which, if properly sharpened, will hold an edge much longer than the typical woodturning tool. Most tools made this way are scraping tools, owing to the limitations of the material thickness and the difficulty in forming the material to a different shape.

1. The three tools shown here have been tipped with sections of planer knives. The width of the tips vary from 3/4" to 3/8".

The handles were purchased but could just as well have been turned to the shape and length one personally prefers.

2. The top row is pieces of planer blade from a surfacer using a segmented head. These sections are very hard, with a Rockwell "C" hardness of about 64. They make very good tip material.

The bottom row is sections cut from an eighteen-inch Tungsten steel jointer blade, and have a Rockwell "C" hardness of about 57. They are a little softer than the sections from the segmented head, but they make excellent tips.

3. One way to make a "tipped" tool is to use 1/2" X 1/2" mild steel square stock and mill or grind a recess to receive the tip.

The top bar has been ground to receive a tip which will be silver soldered into place.

The lower bar has been ground to receive a tip shaped to fit the grind and to be silver soldered into place.

4.   Tips silver soldered in place, and ready for putting into a handle.

Turn a handle to your specifications, drill a hole large enough to accept the bar stock and fill the hole about one-half full of epoxy.

Force the handle into position. The epoxy will flow around the tool, completely filling all voids or cavities.

Wipe off the excess epoxy, set the tool in an upright position, and allow it to cure for twenty-four hours before use.

5.   These tipped bars have been ground to remove flux and roughness left by the silver-soldering operation.

The soldered tips did not lose any of their hardness. They checked out at a Rockwell "C" of 57, the same as before.

6.   Grind the tips to final shape, and leave the wire edge formed during the grinding operation.

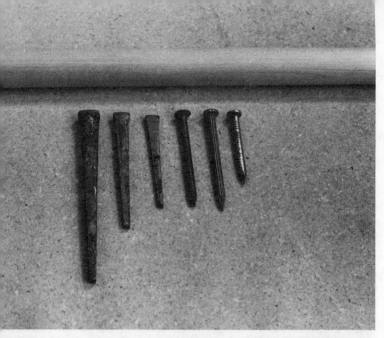

Miniature Tools

1.   Miniature tools are required for fine, delicate turning operations. With a few pieces of dowel rod and some concrete nails, either square cut or round, you have the materials for a good set of tools.

The large square-cut nail is three inches long. It will be used for a skew chisel or a long roundnose.

The other nails are as short as 1¼″ and can be used as required to make the tools you want.

Concrete nails have a Rockwell "C" hardness from 45 to 48—not as hard as one might like, but still hard enough to make a serviceable set of miniature tools.

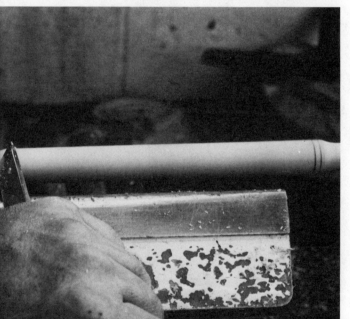

2.   Turn out a set of handles.

I try to keep them about eight inches in length because I like them long enough to be able to use both hands.

I vary the number of rings on each handle. This allows me to identify the tool by looking at the handle, without having to examine the cutting tips, which look similar from a distance.

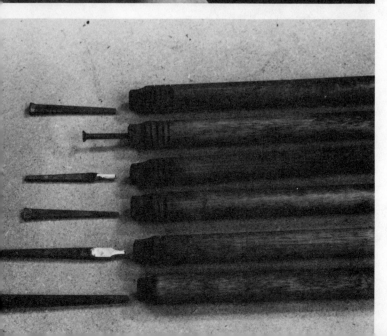

3.   Match the nails to the handles, and drill holes to fit the nails.

Some nails will need to be ground to fit the drilled holes.

Tap the nails into the handles until they are in place and held securely in the handle. You might want to use epoxy as extra precaution.

4. Grind the tools to shape, and polish them. The polishing won't improve the cutting but will certainly help the appearance. In fact, few people will be able to tell that the tools were formerly concrete nails and dowel rod.

The shape of the cutting tip is similar to standard scraping shapes used for wood turning. However, numerous shapes can be ground to fit particular turning requirements.

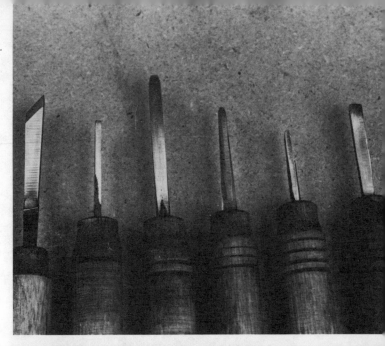

Screw-Center Faceplates

1. Screw-center faceplates are very useful to the woodturner. They can be purchased as an accessory, but they can also be made in the shop. Large screw-center faceplates are particularly useful to the turner who is doing production work and turning bowls and plates.

2. Select a lag bolt or a large wood screw or sheet-metal screw. Use a beveled grinding stone to deepen the threads. This will give the screw center increased holding power. This holding power is particularly important if the faceplate is used for turning green or unseasoned wood, because the regular screws do not hold as well in green wood.

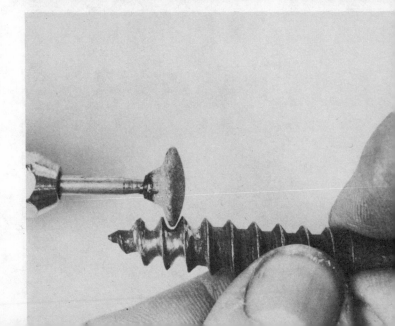

3. If a grinder is not available, a fine-toothed round file will do a good job of increasing the depth of the threads.

4. Note the difference between the depths of the threads that have been deepened and those that have not.

5. Deepen all threads that will protrude through the faceplate.

Grind off the sharp point. The screw will still enter the pilot hole, but the point will not penetrate deeper than necessary.

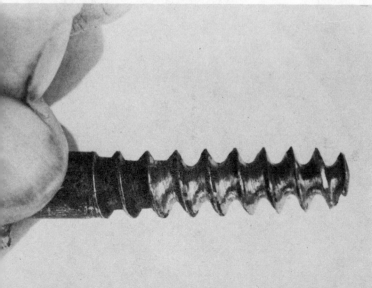

6. This faceplate is about 7/8" thick, and the shank of the lag bolt is 3/8".

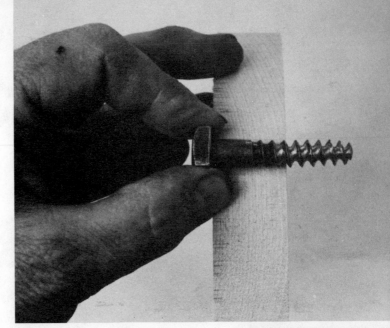

7. Band saw a circular disc about 3/4" to 7/8" thick and a little larger than the metal faceplace.

8. Install the faceplate assembly on the lathe, and drill a pilot hole adequate to receive the screw.

If a chuck is not available to use in boring the hole with the faceplate on the lathe, use a pencil, mark the center point on the spinning disc, and then bore the hole with a hand drill or on the drill press.

It is essential that the hole be accurate, true, and centered in the faceplate.

9. Place a register mark on the wood disc and the metal faceplate.

10. Remove the wooden disc and turn the screw into the hole as far as it will go without stripping the threads.

11. The lag bolt or screw must be pinned to prevent it from turning when stock is being screwed onto the screw center.

Select a bit about 3/32″ in diameter and bore an angled hole through the faceplate and the shank of the bolt.

12. Select a nail of suitable size and drive it into the hole, pinning the screw.

Be careful not to drive the nail out through the face of the faceplate.

Cut off the nail flush with the surface of the faceplate.

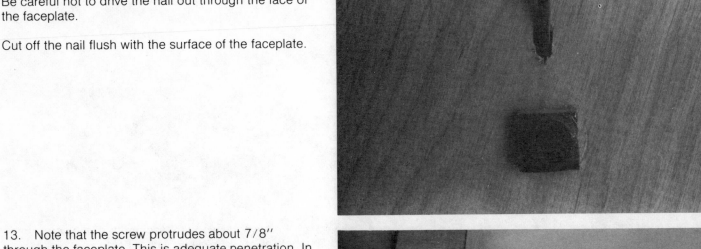

13. Note that the screw protrudes about 7/8″ through the faceplate. This is adequate penetration. In fact, some turnings will require less length, particularly shallow turnings such as plates.

Line up the register marks, and again fasten the wooden faceplate to the metal faceplate. Be sure the screws are tight and secure.

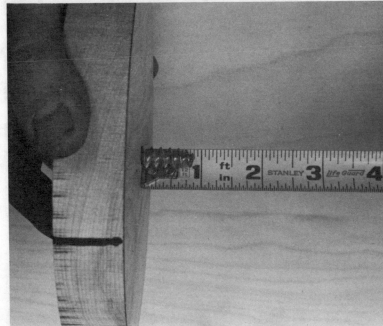

14. Install the faceplate on the lathe, turn the lathe on, and check the screw center to be sure it is turning true.

If it is not turning true, find the off-center side and tap it lightly toward the center of the faceplate.

Check again. The center must turn true.

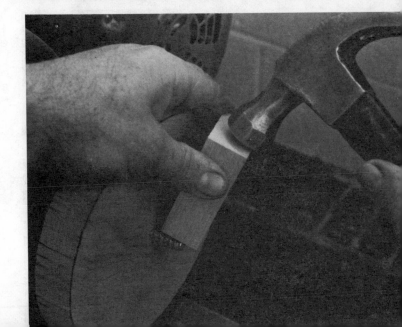

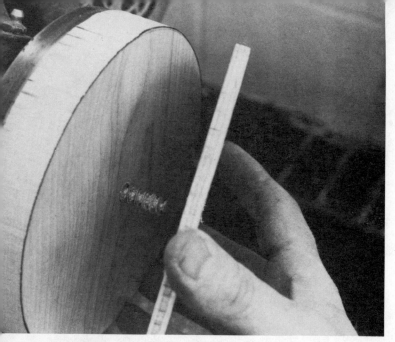

15. Cut out a shim disc for use when less penetration is needed, such as in turning a plate.

Bore a center hole small enough that the disc must be screwed onto the threads.

I make two shim discs, one 1/4″ thick and the other 1/8″ thick. Plywood works well for this. These discs will let me work in 1/8″ steps from 7/8″ maximum screw penetration to 1/2″ minimum. This variation will allow one to do almost any turning normally required.

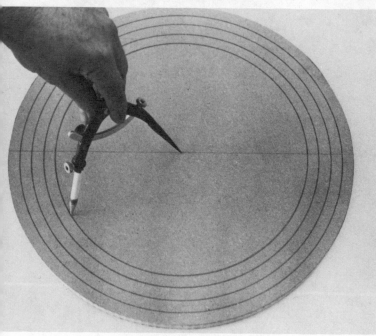

Indexing Unit for Drill Press

Decorative pegging requires precision boring and spacing of holes around a circular object. This can be done several ways, but some are impractical without either a lathe that has an indexing head or a boring machine with its various adjustments. However, most woodturners have access to a drill press, and the following sequence illustrates one way to build an indexing unit for use with a standard drill press. The indexing unit shown in this sequence was used to bore the holes in the turnings shown in decorative pegging sequences in this book. Such a unit is easy to construct and allows holes to be bored with speed and accuracy.

1. Cut out a circular disc equal to the size of the drill press. In this sequence, the disc is made of 3/4″ fiberboard and is fourteen inches in diameter. The disc will become the index wheel.

Lay out a series of circles about 5/8″ apart.

Four circles divided into twenty, twenty-four, thirty, and thirty-six units will give a choice of at least thirteen different spacings.

2. Using a large protractor, divide each circle into the desired number of units.

Tape the protractor in position. Mark one-half of the circle. Turn the protractor over, and do the other half.

Be accurate!

3. The A circle has been divided into thirty-six units of 10 degrees each.

The B circle has been divided into thirty units of 12 degrees each.

The C circle has been divided into twenty-four units of 15 degrees each.

The D circle has been divided into twenty units of 18 degrees each.

Darken each drilling point for easy visibility.

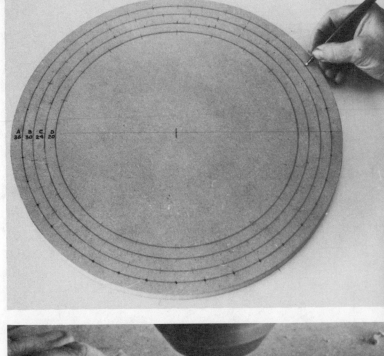

4. Drill a 1/4" hole in the exact center of the index wheel.

5. Select a scrap of plywood, particleboard, or fiberboard large enough to be clamped to the drill-press table. This will function as a temporary base for the index wheel.

Drill a 1/4" hole toward one end of the piece, and drive a short piece of 1/4" rod into the hole.

This rod will act as a pivot point for the index wheel when the indexing holes are drilled.

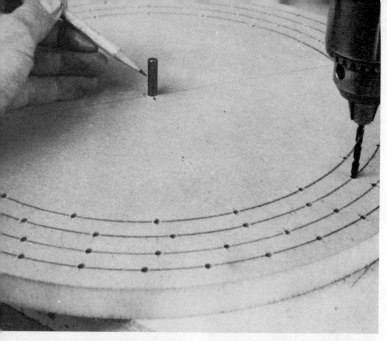

6. Place the index wheel over the 1/4″ rod in the base.

Place the complete unit on the drill-press table, and clamp the base to the table.

The clamping position must allow the index holes to be drilled along each circle.

Drill a series of 1/8″ holes through the index wheel, using the layout points for positioning the holes.

Be accurate!

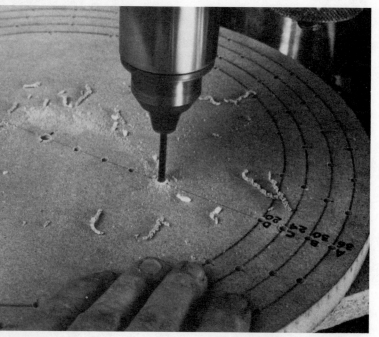

7. Remove the index wheel from the temporary base, and drill three or four 1/8″ holes through the index wheel as shown.

These holes will be used to fasten the rough turning to the index wheel using 1¼″ screws.

8. Turn the index wheel over, and countersink the screw holes.

The countersunk holes must be deep enough to allow the screw head to be set below the surface of the wheel.

9. Select a piece of stock for the permanent base, and install a 1/4'' pivot pin.

The pin must extend above the base at least 1¼'', assuming the index wheel is 3/4'' thick.

Position the index wheel on the base as shown, and clamp the wheel to the base.

Drill holes at each point marked A, B, C or D, using the holes in the index wheel as guides.

These holes should go through the base piece; they will function as indexing points for holding the index pin.

10. The index pin shown in the hole at point A is made from a duplex head nail, with the point ground to a long taper.

The pencil points to the screw used for fastening the turning to the index wheel.

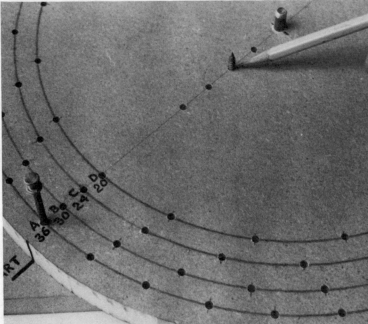

11. The completed index wheel may be finished with a clear lacquer or other finish to protect the surface during use.

The setup and use of the index wheel is further explained in the sequence ''Decorative Pegging with Oak Branch Pegs.''

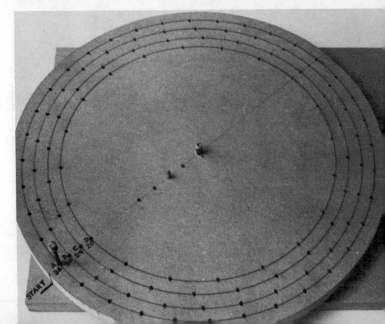

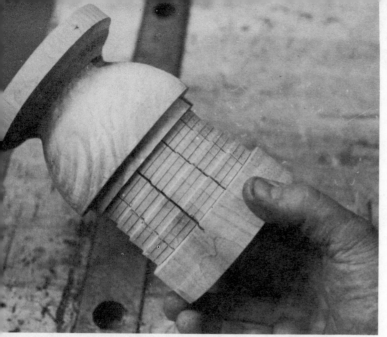

The Step-Tapered Circular Chuck

1. The step-tapered circular chuck is used to hold small boxes so a foot can be turned on the base of the box. The chuck can be compressed to allow the box to fit the correct-sized step, and the spring pressure will hold the box in place. The shoulder on the step allows the box to be positioned parallel to the face plate and to turn true without wobbling or being off center.

2. Select a piece of hardwood such as maple or birch. The stock should be about three to four inches long and a little thicker than the largest diameter needed for the chuck. The piece must be turned with the end-grain against the faceplate to allow the chuck to have side or edge grain around the perimeter. The fingers of the chuck must be strong but flexible; therefore, end-grain can appear only on the ends of the chuck.

Band saw the stock to rough shape, and mount the stock to a faceplate. I use a screw center for convenience, but the stock could be mounted to a regular faceplate and left permanently fastened for future use.

3. Turn the stock to rough shape.

For a chuck with five or six steps of about 1/16″ each, turn the first step with a shoulder about 3/8″ wide and 3/8″ deep.

4. Make each step 3/8" wide and 1/16" deep. The series of steps will move back toward the base of the chuck in 3/8" X 1/16" increments.

I find that five or six steps is enough for one chuck. If more variation in size is needed, make another chuck.

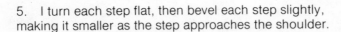

5. I turn each step flat, then bevel each step slightly, making it smaller as the step approaches the shoulder.

Beveling the step slightly allows the pressure to be exerted at a point down inside the box, and seems to produce a more secure fit.

Leave the steps in rough condition. The rough fibers will help hold the box securely.

6. Hollow out the interior of the chuck, leaving a wall thickness of about 1/8".

The depth of the interior should be about 1/4" past the last step.

Walls that are too thick will make a chuck that is stiff and rigid, with little flexibility. Walls that are too thin will make a chuck that is limber and will not hold the box securely.

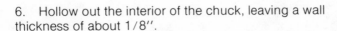

7. When the chuck has been turned to shape and hollowed out, I make two V grooves on each step. The grooves are shallow and left rough, but they seem to improve the holding power of the chuck.

8. Place the chuck in a vise and make a series of cuts down through the last step.

I usually make the cuts to produce eight or twelve equal-sized fingers on the chuck.

More cuts make a chuck flexible; fewer cuts, a chuck that is more rigid.

9. This chuck has a wall thickness of a little less than 1/8″. It has twelve fingers.

The small step diameter is about three inches; the largest step diameter, 3 5/16″.

I have several chucks similar to this one, some larger and some smaller.

This type of chuck works very well if the inside of the turning is straight.

Figured tulipwood. Ed Moulthrop. *Photo by Gabriel Benzur.*

Turning a Bowl from Unseasoned Wood

A bowl may be turned from wood that is freshly cut, or from wood in various stages of seasoning. The turning procedures are the same, except that the fresh cut, or green, wood will turn more easily, and tools will stay sharp longer. In addition the bowl may need to be treated differently at the end of the rough turning. It is very difficult to rough turn all the bowls when wood is green, because even a small log may yield a hundred or more bowls of various sizes. I work with wood in all stages of seasoning, but I prefer to work with green wood: It turns quickly and easily.

1.   Lay out the bowl to the best advantage, taking into account figure, defects, size, and waste.

Often, small bowls and large bowls can be efficiently laid out on the rough stock.

2.   Cut the bowl blanks to rough shape on the band saw.

3.   A blank cut with straight sides will allow the turner more flexibility in the shape of the turning, but it wastes more wood than does a blank with beveled sides.

4. If a bowl allows it, tilt the band-saw table and cut out a rough blank with beveled sides.

The angle cut will allow the bowl to be turned in less time, as part of the waste is removed with the saw.

The waste stock can be used for small turnings, as the pieces are often quite large and of usable size.

5. This faceplate is being fastened to the base of the bowl with 7/8" #14 sheet-metal screws.

These screws hold better in unseasoned wood than do standard wood screws. And because the sheet-metal screws are hardened, the heads will not deform easily, which means that the screws can be used many times.

6. Install the faceplate and bowl blank on the head stock.

Move the tailstock into position and clamp it to the lathe bed.

Advance the dead center into firm contact with the bowl blank. This is a safety precaution, and it helps eliminate vibration when the outside of the bowl is being turned to shape.

7. I bring the bowl into round by using a modified square-nose chisel with a scraping action.

This may not be a beautiful way to turn, but it is certainly fast and efficient.

8.   Make several cuts to rough shape the bowl. The shavings will come off in ribbons, and 1/4" or more wood can be removed with each pass.

The amount which can be removed depends on the power of the lathe, the sharpness of the tool, the condition of the wood, and (as usual) the skill of the turner.

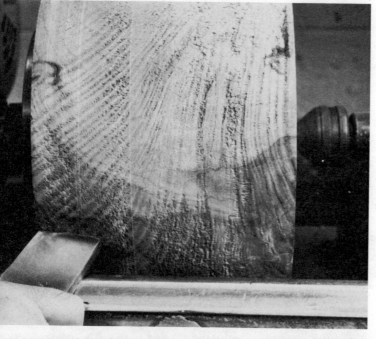

9.   The modified square-nose chisel does not cut clean; rather, a scraping action is involved.

Usually, a 1/8" shearing cut with a gouge will clean up the surface, and leave it in good condition.

10.   A deep-fluted gouge is used for turning the bowl to final shape.

Position the gouge with the handle down and resting against your body, with the gouge partially rolled over toward the direction of cut.

The full bevel of the gouge should be in contact with the stock. The depth of cut is established and maintained by the bevel rubbing against the turning.

Proper gouge action will cut shavings from the stock. Dust or sawdust particles indicate scraping action.

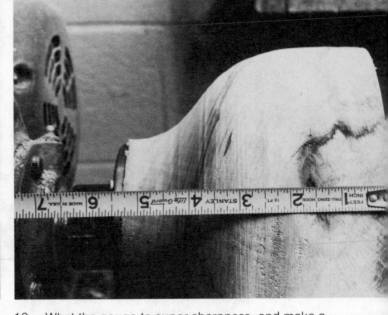

11.   Skillful use of the gouge requires a lot of practice but, when mastered, is a very rewarding way to turn.

Here the cut being made is coming back against the grain. However, it is easier and better to cut from the large diameter toward the small diameter or, to say it another way, "downhill."

Cutting downhill will give a smooth, even surface, with minimal tearing, because the cut is being made with the grain of the wood.

12.   Keep the tool rest close to the work, usually within 1/4" to 1/2". This is particularly important when using a gouge and making a shearing cut.

13.   Whet the gouge to super sharpness, and make a light final cut.

This should leave a very good surface.

14.   Measure the thickness of the bowl.

15.   Measure back on the drill bit, and make a mark allowing for approximately one inch of wood to be left in the bottom of the bowl.

A multispur bit cuts clean and fast and leaves a flat-bottomed hole.

16.   Boring the hole establishes the depth of the bowl, so one need not check the depth continually during the turning process, and it removes the center core, which is more difficult to remove than other areas.

Bore the center hole into the stock.

Do not go too deep.

This operation can also be done on a drill press, or with a portable hand drill.

17.   The interior of the bowl can be shaped using scraping or cutting tools. The remainder of this sequence illustrates the use of a deep gouge for turning the interior of a bowl.

The basic position I use is to place my left hand on the tool rest, so that I can control the movement of the gouge, and my right hand over the handle of the gouge and resting on the lathe bed.

The right hand actually works as a pivot point, with the gouge sweeping an arc from the outer edge of the bowl into the center.

18.   Determining the point of entry on the outer rim is the most difficult part to master.

I lay the gouge on its back in scraping position and then enter the stock.

41

19.   As the gouge enters the stock, slowly roll the gouge as shown, at the same time starting the sweep toward the center of the bowl.

20.   Roll the gouge until the full angle of the bevel is rubbing, but not so far as to allow the corner of the gouge to dig into the wood.

Continue the sweep toward the center of the bowl, removing as much stock as you feel comfortable with.

21.   As you approach the center of the turning, roll the gouge back a little, and complete the sweep.

If the sweep has been well done, the motion is continuous from beginning to end, with shavings flowing in a continuous stream from the cutting edge of the gouge.

This is turning at its best—the feeling of enjoyment and satisfaction that comes from mastering a difficult skill.

22.   As the turning progresses, continue to move the tool rest into the bowl, keeping it as close to the work as possible.

This turning is almost complete.

23. Sharpen a large roundnose and leave the burr or wire edge on.

Make the final shaping and the clean-up cuts.

24. This bowl has been turned to final shape. The wall thickness is a uniform 3/4". Because the wood was partially seasoned, less wall thickness was required. If the wood had been green, the wall should have been a uniform 1", to allow for greater distortion when drying. For large bowls, I often leave a wall thickness of 1¼" to 1½".

25. In Utah (a dry, hot area) it is necessary to coat the bowl inside and out with a thick layer of paste wax. However, if you live in cooler, more humid areas, this treatment may not be essential. For a detailed discussion of the treatment of green wood, see ''Harvesting Green Wood.''

Place the bowl on the floor in a cool area, away from air movement and high temperatures.

Seasoning should be complete in four to six months.

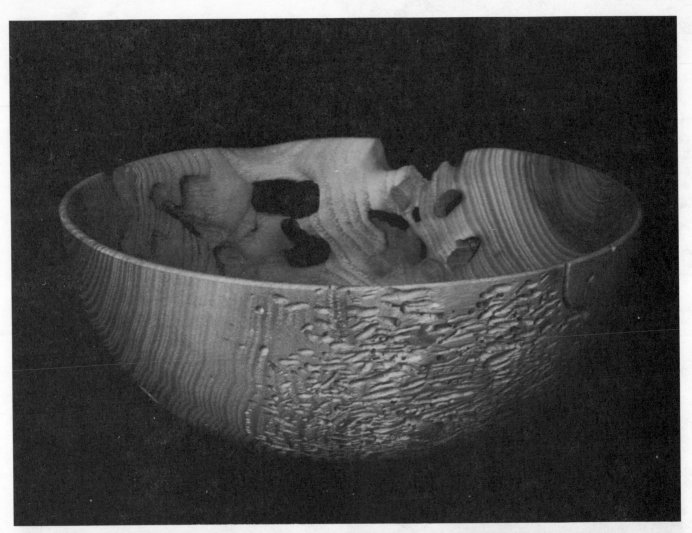

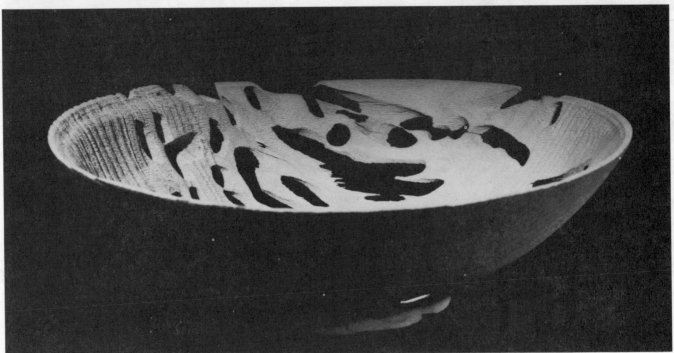

Wormy ash bowls. Dale L. Nish.

Bowls from "Wormy" Wood

Over the years, as I have selected wood for turning, I have noticed in myself a gradual change in interest and willingness to collect the unusual piece of wood for whatever reason made it unique. At one time I would consider only the sound, seasoned piece free from defects such as decay, knots, bark pockets, and stain. I would never have considered using a piece of wood containing beetles and borers; these were problems the woodworker avoided like a disease. However, the problems created by beetles and borers can be the source of very interesting one-of-a-kind turnings. Some will say, "That's not for me". So be it. But others will accept this sequence as an opportunity to try something different.

1.   This bowl has enough "defects" to have been rejected several times over. It has checked knots, discoloration, and evidence of powder-post beetles and wood borers.

However, it is also a challenging, one-of-a-kind turning. For that reason it could have been sold many times.

2.   These planks were severely infested with beetles and borers, and were first tossed into the firewood pile.

Later, a single bowl was turned to see what it would look like.

The following sequence is the story of a similar bowl.

3.   The top area in the plank, which was exposed to the outside of the pile, is drier and has become a home for the powder-post beetle.

The bottom area of the plank remained moist and has been taken over by the wood borers.

The plank also has other defects, but it is an interesting challenge.

4. Band saw the bowl blank to shape, drill a pilot hole, and mount the blank on a screw-center faceplate.

Move the tailstock into position to support the turning while it is being roughed out.

5. Rough shape the outside of the bowl using a gouge or roundnose.

Sharpen the tool, and make a final light finishing cut.

6. Notice the effects of the borers activities in this section of the bowl.

7. An interesting part of the bowl, but to some, a cause for discarding the piece.

8. When the bowl has been shaped, move the tailstock back and face off the base of the bowl.

9. A small drill with a three-inch-diameter flexible abrasive disc makes it very easy to sand the turning.

The rubber support allows the disc to flex and sand the curves on the turning, and the rotating action keeps the abrasive cool and clean. My experience is that one three-inch disc will sand longer and better than several sheets of paper.

Another advantage of the disc is that it will bridge the open areas and, if used properly, will seldom catch on a ragged piece of stock.

Before attempting to sand the piece with the lathe rotating the stock, practice control with the lathe stopped.

Most bowls can be sanded completely with the use of 60, 80, 100, and 150 grit discs.

10. Sand the base with the tool held as shown.

Work the edge of the disc into the sharp curve where the base joins the bowl.

The flexible action should produce a pleasing curve, but be careful that the edge of the disc does not cut into the bowl and leave a groove.

Don't allow the drill to get trapped between the turning and the lathe bed.

11. When sanding is complete, mount the piece using a three-jaw chuck, or (if the chuck is not available) use a block glued to the base and fasten it to a regular faceplate.

The easiest way to align the block is to glue it to the base while the bowl is still mounted on the screw-center faceplate. When the glue has set, turn the block down to the diameter of the faceplate to which it is to be fastened. Then, keeping the block and faceplate in alignment, put in the screws. This will give almost perfect registration and alignment.

12. Tape the outside of the bowl where the beetles and borers have worked, as well as other places that may be weak because of decay or checking.

These must be taped to provide support while the inside is being turned. This is also a safety precaution—to prevent a piece from breaking off and striking the turner. Several layers of tape may be needed, and they should be well overlapped onto the sound areas of the bowl.

13. Rough out the interior of the bowl as shown, but do not remove too much wood.

At this time, the wall thickness should be about 5/16" to 3/8" thick, and down 1" to 1½" into the bowl.

Use a sharp tool and make a final finishing cut, leaving the wall about 1/8" to 3/16" thick.

The secret of turning a thin wall, free from vibration, is to turn from the thin wood to the heavy wood in steps of 1" to 1½".

I use a sharp gouge and a shearing cut to make the finished surface.

14. This piece has a finished wall down to the area of the base.

15. Use a roundnose, and remove most of the stock from the inside of the bowl.

Leave a small post for support, then undercut it and break it off.

16. Complete the turning of the inside of the bowl.

17. The bowl completely shaped, ready for sanding.

18. Sanding the interior of the bowl is done with the abrasive disc and with the lathe running at low speed.

Again, practice control with the lathe stopped. When you feel comfortable in handling the drill and rotating disc, proceed with the sanding.

Never let the top edge of the disc contact the spinning bowl. Sand with the bottom half of the disc, and hold the drill securely.

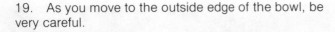

19. As you move to the outside edge of the bowl, be very careful.

Exert light pressure. Stop immediately if a piece of wood comes loose, the tape starts to flap, or the bowl grabs the disc. All of these indicate problems.

Stop the lathe, carefully examine the piece, and take the steps necessary to remedy the problem before continuing with the sanding.

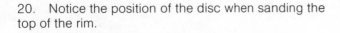

20. Notice the position of the disc when sanding the top of the rim.

Keep the top edge of the disc well away from the turning, and sand with light pressure because the walls are fragile and may be ragged.

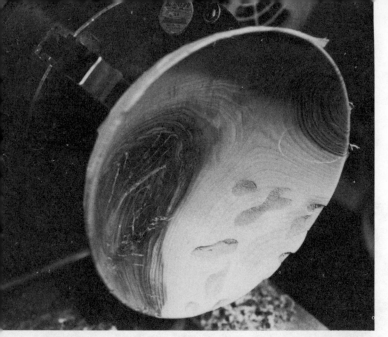

21. The sanded bowl ready for finishing.

22. One method of finishing is to sandblast the holes and checks to remove dirt and the castings of the borers and beetles. This process may also be used to give a pleasing texture to the wood.

Sandblasting and the turning process should remove all beetles and borers from the wood. As a final precaution, however, I place the turning in a microwave oven and turn it on for a few seconds, the time depending on the size of the turning. This technique quickly eliminates any remaining insect life.

Black walnut. Dale L. Nish.

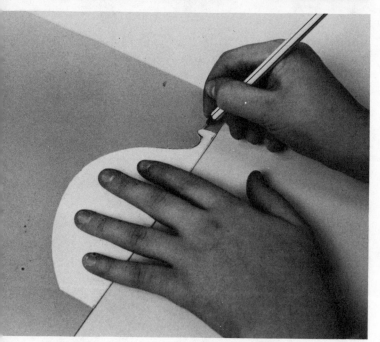

Enclosed Containers

Enclosed containers are turnings with small openings that make them difficult, if not impossible, to hollow out. In the past, most of this style of turning has been turned to an external shape suitable to the designer or turner, with little regard for the internal shape of the piece. Typically a turning has been vase shaped, with a hole bored into the piece to allow it to hold decorative articles such as flowers. It has always dismayed me to pick up a piece that has a fragile, delicate appearance, but feels like a chunk of wood. I feel the shape should be complemented by an esthetic of touch or feel. One should not detract from the other. As a result, I have developed a method for hollowing out a container and turning a piece that feels as it looks. The following pictures and notes illustrate one technique. I am sure there are others.

1. Sketch a shape that will satisfy you.

Play with variations of the original idea until you are satisfied.

Try to select a shape that can be turned from a single solid block of wood.

2. Fold the shape down the center line, and cut it out the same way you would cut out a valentine.

Slip a piece of cardboard into the fold and trace one-half of the shape onto the cardboard.

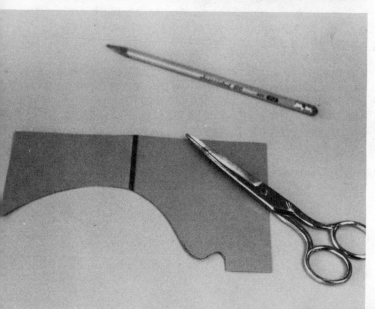

3. Cut out the interior of the shape, and select the place where a parting line is desired. Later this line will be used as part of the decoration of the piece, and will be emphasized as part of the design.

Mark a dark line 1/8'' wide at the parting point.

Cut the pattern along the edge of the line, then cut the line from the other part of the pattern. This allows the pattern to compensate for the wood removed by the parting tool when the piece is being separated.

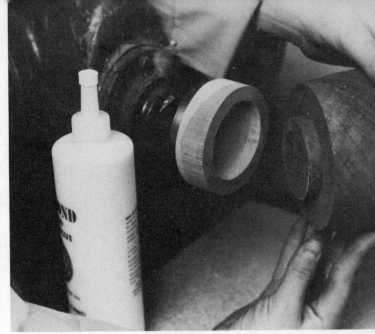
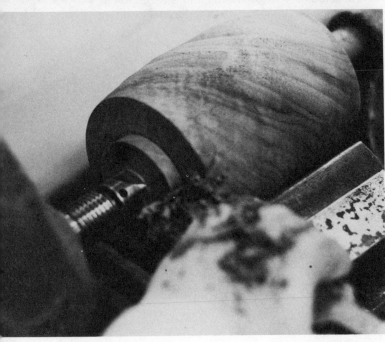

4.   Select a solid block of wood of a size suitable for the turning.

Place it between centers, and turn it to a rough cylinder. You may use a gouge (as shown), a roundnose, or modified square-nose. The idea is to remove the wood as efficiently as you can.

5.   Turn a dowel on one end of the cylinder. Keep the dowel smaller than the base of the completed turning. A square-nose does a good job of this.

6.   Fasten a wooden disc to a regular faceplate, and bore a hole to accept the dowel on the cylinder. This should be a good fit.

The depth of the hole should be 1/16'' more than the length of the dowel. This will allow the dowel to be forced in until the shoulders hit the disc. At the same time glue will adhere the end of the dowel to the disc, helping to strengthen the joint.

7.   Spread glue inside the hole in the disc and over and around the dowel, being sure to be generous around the shoulders of the dowel.

Insert the dowel into the disc and clamp firmly. The lathe makes a good clamp.

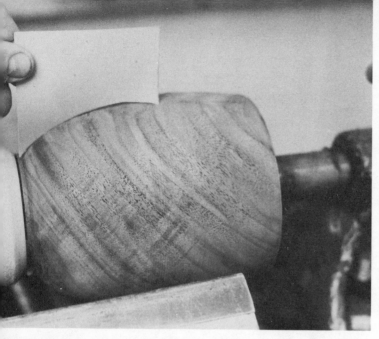

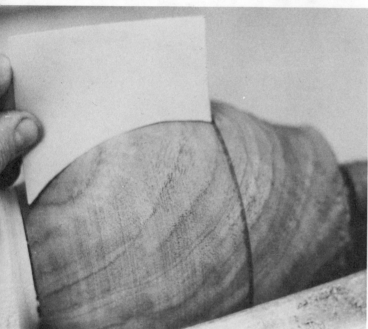

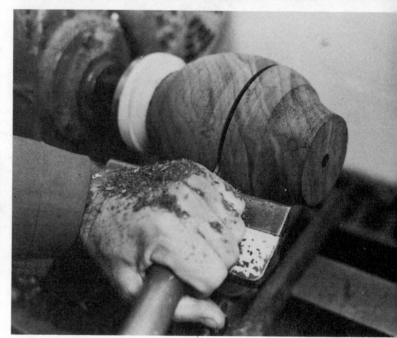

8. Turn the cylinder to the rough shape of the pattern. Remember, the base is against the faceplate.

Check periodically, and continue turning until the pattern fits.

9. Mark the parting line, and turn off about 1/8" of wood, starting at the base and stopping at the parting line.

Check with the pattern to be sure the basic shape is kept.

The extra wood on the top part will be needed to compensate for the change in the turning when it is separated into two pieces.

10. Bore a hole in the top piece.

The hole should be 3/8" or 1/2" in diameter, depending on dowels available, and about two inches deep.

11. Using a parting tool, cut into the turning at the parting line. You will be cutting deeply, so be careful that the tool does not catch in the wood.

It may be wise to widen the cut slightly, but do not change the cutting angle.

The cutting angle should be about 10 degrees and should slope toward the bottom of the turning.

Run the lathe at a slow speed.

 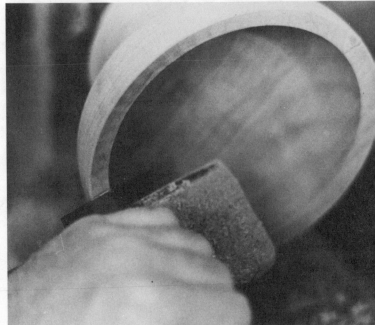

12. When you feel the top part vibrate slightly, or when the sound of the cutting action changes to a higher pitch, stop the lathe and break the top part loose from the base.

A twisting action will do this.

13. Use a multispur bit and bore a depth hole to within 1″ of the bottom of the turning.

This will remove the center part and will be an indicator of when the rough bottom is reached. The depth hole saves time and effort.

14. Remove the interior of the base part, using a tool you are comfortable with. I commonly use a gouge or roundnose.

Leave 1/2″ to 5/8″ of wood in the bottom and keep the walls 1/2″ at the bottom, tapering to 3/8″ at the top.

15. True up the edge of the bevel.

Try not to change the angle, but the edge must be clean and true.

16. Check for straightness, using a straightedge.

It is essential that this edge be true and flat.

17. Fasten a round disc to a faceplate, and bore a hole the same size as the hole previously drilled in the top part of the turning.

18. Place a dowel in the hole, and glue it in.

The dowel serves as an alignment pin to keep the stock in correct position on the faceplate.

19. Place glue in the hole in the top part, as well as around the flat area.

Glue the two pieces together. The lathe makes a good clamp.

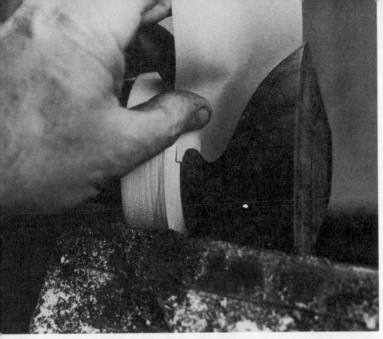

20. Turn the outside of the top piece to rough shape. Check with the pattern, keeping in mind that the neck will not be turned until later.

Do not get the neck area too small, but be sure the rest of the top part is to the correct shape.

21. Rough out the inside of the top piece, keeping a uniform wall thickness of about 3/8".

22. Select a bit the diameter of the smallest interior part of the neck, and bore a hole through the top piece.

23. Complete the inside turning, and sand to a suitable finish.

If you are careful, a fine finish cut with a roundnose or gouge is a suitable finish for the interior.

Using a parting tool, partially separate the top part from the disc.

When the top part begins to vibrate, stop the lathe and twist the top part from the disc.

24. Check the fit of the top part to the bottom. If necessary, place the bottom part on the lathe, and fit it to the top part.

The bevels should contact at the outside of the turning and be slightly open on the inside. This will allow a very tight joint at the outside diameter of the turning.

Line up the top and bottom parts so the grain pattern matches as closely as possible.

Using an aliphatic base glue, such as Titebond, glue the two parts together.

Use the lathe as a clamp, but do not apply too much pressure, because that might crack the turning.

Let the assembly cure overnight.

25. Face off the neck of the turning, and turn the neck to rough shape.

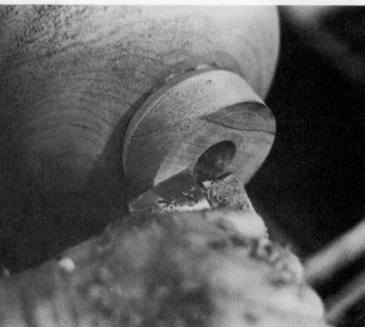

26. Continue to refine the shape, blending the lines to their final contours.

Remember, only about 1/8" can be removed without weakening the wall or turning through the piece and ruining it.

Turn at a low speed, not more than 650 to 800 rpm, depending on the size of the turning.

27. Remove the turning from the lathe, and examine the lines carefully.

It is best to stand the turning up in a normal position, and view it from different angles.

28. Make any final shape adjustments, such as smoothing a line or making the neck smaller.

29. After the exterior has been shaped, use a small roundnose and gently finish the interior of the neck.

Take a light cut, use a sharp tool, and prevent chatter or vibration.

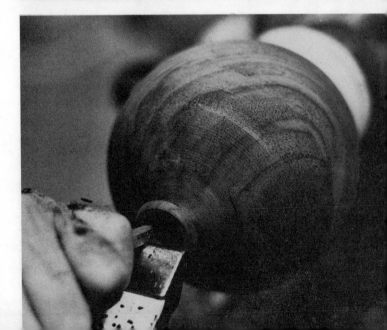

30. Outline the shoulder of the turning with a parting tool.

Be sure the tool is sharp.

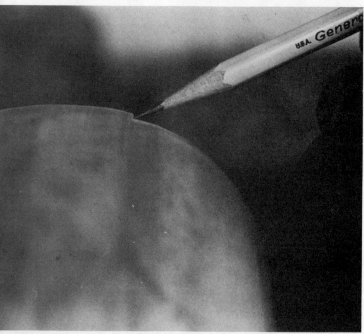

31. On this turning the shoulder is inset about 1/8". Later this area will be hand carved.

32. Outline a similar shoulder at the base of the neck. Blend the area into the shape of the turning.

33. A close-up of the neck.

Notice the gentle shaping and blending of the curved areas.

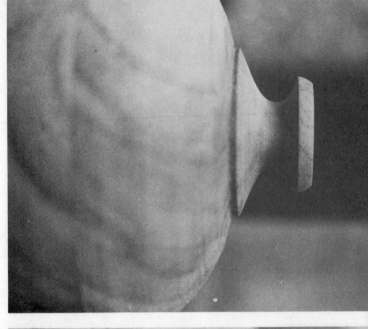

34. A close-up of the neck opening. The surfaces make a gentle transition into the opening, which is actually smaller than it appears.

35. Using a parting tool, partially separate the turning from the disc.

Cut in 1/2" to 3/4".

The cut will be completed later on the band saw.

36.   Sand the turning as desired. On this turning, the part between the shoulders is not sanded, because it will be carved later.

Note the steel wool between pieces of abrasive paper. This helps keep the fingers cool, and gives uniform pressure over a larger sanding area.

Black walnut. Dale L. Nish.

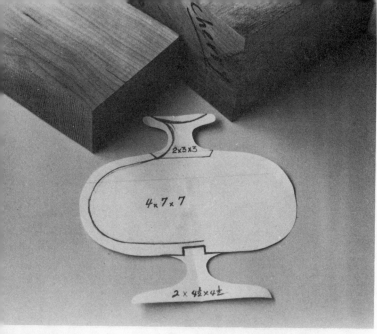

Footed Vase

1. Using the valentine method, cut out a shape desired for the particular turning.

Keep in mind restrictions such as available material and lathe capacity.

Notice that the turning will be made from three pieces:
one 2" X 3" X 3" for the top,
one 4" X 7" X 7" for the body, and
one 2" X 4½" X 4½" for the foot.

2. Mount the body to a faceplate. For this turning I glued the body to a disc and screwed the faceplate to the disc. This prevented the screw hole from appearing in the body of the turning.

Bore a 1¼" diameter X 1/2" deep hole. The size of this hole is not critical, but do not bore into the part that later will be inside of the vase.

Rough turn the body to the required shape. I am using a gouge in this picture.

3. Use a roundnose next to the faceplate. You will have better control, and there is less chance that the tool will grab or run.

4.   Glue the base of the turning to a smaller disc, and fasten the disc to a faceplate.

Turn a dowel on the end of the base piece. This dowel must fit into the bottom of the body of the vase.

5.   Turn the shoulder of the base to a diameter equal to the flat part on the body piece.

Check for a good fit.

6.   Glue the body and the base piece together.

Use the lathe as a clamp.

Let dry overnight.

7.   Check the pattern, and turn the opening into the top of the body to receive the top piece.

The side of the opening should be beveled toward the center at about a 10-degree angle.

The depth of this hole is not critical; later we will turn up into it.

8. Glue the top piece to a disc, and fasten the disc to a faceplate.

Carefully fit the shoulder of the top piece to the angle of the opening in the body.

This must be a very good fit.

9. Glue the top piece into the body of the vase.

Clamp and leave until the glue has set.

10. Turn the outside of the turning to rough shape. Use a gouge or roundnose.

Leave a shoulder at the point where the parting tool will be used to separate the top of the vase from the base.

11. With the parting tool, cut into the turning at the parting line. You will be cutting deeply, so widen the cut slightly to help prevent the tool from catching in the wood.

Try to maintain a cutting angle of 10–15 degrees sloping toward the bottom of the body.

When the top piece begins to vibrate slightly, stop the lathe and twist the top piece, separating it from the other part of the turning.

Hollow out the base of the body in the usual manner.

12. Turn the top part of the vase to rough shape.

A gouge works well on the interior.

Turn the outside to finished shape, but do not turn the top piece.

In this photo, the top part is held in a three-jaw chuck, but it could be held using other methods.

13. Bore a hole through the top piece, using a bit the size of the narrowest part of the opening.

Blend the interior of the top piece into the hole, leaving a wall thickness of 1/4'' to 3/8''.

14.   True up the beveled edge.

Maintaining the correct angle, cut the edge clean and flat.

15.   Glue the two pieces together.

The glue should bead around the edge, indicating adequate glue for a strong joint.

Exert a firm, but not excessive clamping pressure.

16.   Rough shape the top of the vase, using a sharp roundnose chisel.

Take light cuts, and prevent vibration.

If necessary, move the dead center up against the end of the top, and lightly contact the end of the turning. If you are handling the tool properly, this will reduce vibration problems.

17. Use the same bit as was used to bore the interior hole in the top (see Figure 13).

Bore into the top piece until the bit passes through the interior hole.

18. Shape the exterior to final form.

If possible, use a gouge to clean up the large surfaces.

Use a roundnose on the smaller areas.

Remember, only about 1/8″ of wood can be removed without weakening the walls or turning through the piece.

19. To conceal the parting line, I chose to make a change in shape at that point. A shallow cut with the roundnose leaves a small cove ending at the edge of the parting line.

Another small cove defines the base of the top.

The area between the coves will be textured later.

20. The base was shaped with a roundnose, and a flat shoulder was turned at the point where the base was glued to the body. This effectively conceals the joint.

With a parting tool, partially separate the base from the disc.

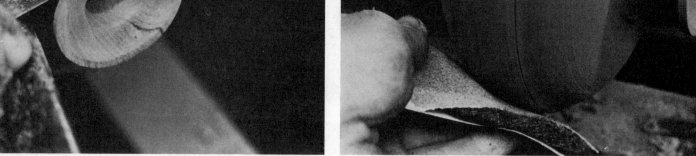

21.   A close-up of the finished base.

Note that the rim of the foot was rounded sightly and was reduced in size at the bottom. This gives the foot a lighter appearance.

22.   Make the final shaping cuts on the top.

Use a sharp roundnose, and take a light cut.

23.   The finished top.

Note the repetition of form in the top and the base.

24.   Sand the vase.

I recommend finishing with a 220 grit paper.

Note the steel wool pad, which is used to distribute pressure and to protect the fingers from the heat.

Box elder and walnut. Dale L. Nish.

Laminated Bowls (Flat Stock)

1.   Select several pieces of stock of the desired thickness and size to produce the turning.

This basic assembly consists of two pieces of box elder, two pieces of shedua, and one piece of walnut.

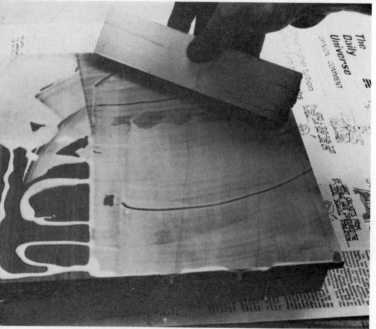

2.   Spread a thin, even coat on each contact surface.

Assemble the lamination, and clamp it up with a firm, even pressure.

Equal pressure distribution is very important. There must be no starved areas or glue pockets.

A press or sandbagging will work best, but parallel clamps can be used if the surface is not too large for the clamps to reach to the center of the assembly.

3.   Trim the edges of the assembly until they are true and square.

One option (to be shown in the sequence) is to cut a wedge off one side and glue it on the other side, giving the appearance of an angled lamination.

Make certain that both outside surfaces are true and flat.

Tilt the band saw to the desired angle, and, using a sharp blade, cut off a wedge.

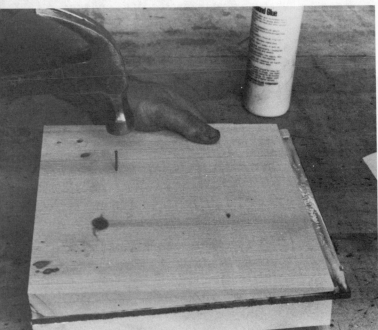

4.   Spread the glue on the contact surfaces.

Here a piece of walnut is placed between the wedge piece and the basic assembly.

5.   Tack the wedge into position. Place the nails so that the holes will be removed during the turning of the bowl.

The wedge surface will become the top of the bowl. This will place the three dark pieces in the bottom of the bowl, giving it an appearance of stability.

6.   Clamp the wedge and walnut piece into position and let cure overnight.

When cured, cut out the blank on the band saw.

7.   I glue a waste piece to the bottom of the bowl, to allow the faceplate screws to be set into the waste piece, rather than having holes in the bottom of the turning.

Turn the piece to shape and wall thickness, using the same technique used for turning solid stock.

8.   A sharp roundnose works best on the interior of the bowl, particularly if the bowl has a concave interior edge on the lip of the bowl.

The angle of the pieces will give some pleasant surprises.

9.   The exterior appearance is one of motion and action, owing to the angles of the laminations and to the exterior shape of the turning. I try to keep the shape simple so as not to detract from the interest produced by the laminations.

10.   The interior of the bowl gives the appearance of being out-of-round. However, this adds to the interest and motion exhibited by the turning. Leaving the white wood in the bottom of the bowl gives the turning an appearance of added depth and dimension, as well as displaying the angular surfaces of the other layers of wood.

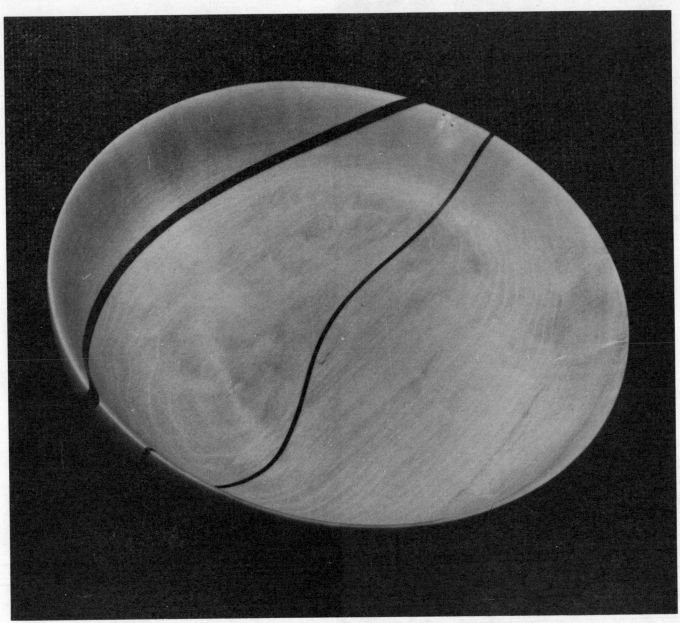

Box elder and walnut. Dale L. Nish.

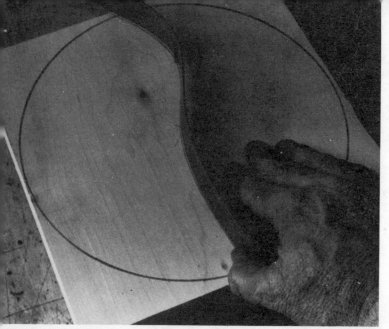

Laminated Bowls (Free-Form Inserts)

One often encounters a piece of stock with a plain, uninteresting figure that offers little incentive for turning. A way to add interest and numerous design options is to cut the piece apart and add contrasting inserts, producing a laminated blank of one's choice. I might give a caution here, because there is a tendency to become too enthusiastic, adding inserts until the piece becomes a design monstrosity. I prefer simplicity, using the inserts to provide points of accent and interest, but not so that they dominate the natural appearance of the piece. Use the inserts to add movement and depth to the piece, but use them sparingly.

The inserts may contrast with the piece, or blend in with more subtle tones. Used in accordance with good design principles, the inserts may add quiet elegance to a piece which would have been rather ordinary had it been turned as solid stock.

1. Select a piece of solid stock of the desired color and thickness. The piece can contrast with the inserts or blend with them, the inserts acting as subtle accents.

Draw a circle on the face of the stock and lay out a free-form curve across the piece. I use finish nails driven into the piece to determine the points where the curves change direction.

Use the finish nails as guides, and use a piece of veneer to make the curves.

Trace the desired curve on the stock.

2. Using a sharp band saw, carefully cut the stock in two.

If the saw cut is clean and true to the line, there will be no need to true it up later.

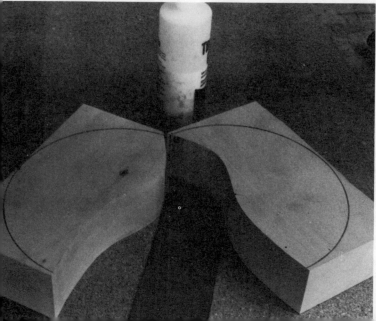

3. The insert is a thin piece of veneer. If more thickness is desired, use several pieces. Several thin pieces will bend more easily than one thick piece.

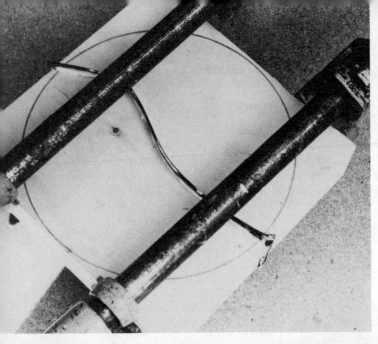

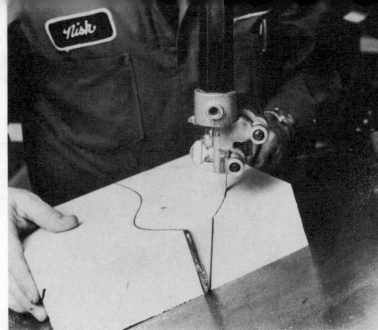

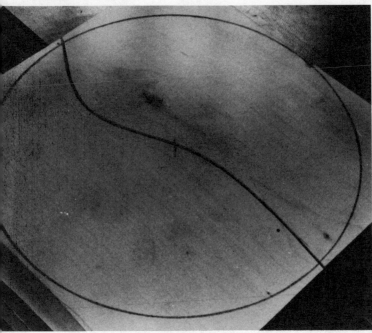

4.   Spread glue on all surfaces, clamp the assembly securely, and let it set overnight.

5.   Using a plane or sharp chisel, remove the excess insert and glue before laying out any other desired free-form curve.

6.   Another curve has been laid out, and for a variation in form the saw table has been tilted to give an angle cut to the piece.

7.   The second insert will be thicker than the first; therefore, a small amount of wood must be taken from both sides of the saw cut to make the curves parallel to each other when the insert is in place.

A good way to accomplish this is with a belt sander.

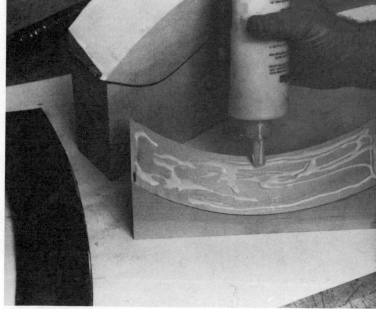

8. Sand both the inside and the outside curves accurately and smooth.

Check the two pieces for fit, and make the necessary adjustments.

9. Place a small piece of veneer between the two pieces, and trace a line on the veneer along both sides of the stock.

This piece will be the pattern for the insert pieces.

10. Cut out several pieces of veneer to build up the required thickness of the insert.

The pieces will not be straight, because they are being fit into a compound curve.

11. Place glue on the contact surfaces, and spread it out in a thin, uniform coat.

A thin coat on each surface is better than a thick coat on one surface.

12. Place the insert in position and clamp one end, using just enough pressure to pull the assembly together.

Use a chisel to cut the insert down flush with the main piece. Do this on both sides.

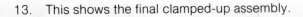

Place a C clamp in position to hold the insert in place, and to prevent the assembly from sliding when it is clamped up.

Change ends with the bar clamp, and repeat the above steps on the other end of the insert.

13. This shows the final clamped-up assembly.

Note the two bar clamps on the bottom, as well as the one on the top. These give good clamping pressure, and they keep the laminated assembly flat.

Because the cut is on an angle, the two C clamps are necessary to keep the pieces from sliding. If it were a straight cut, the C clamps would not be necessary.

14. The completed lamination has been planed flat and true.

Lay out the desired bowl size, and cut it out on the band saw.

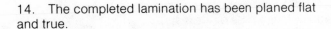

15. The laminated bowl is turned the same as if it were a solid piece of stock. The inserts do not present any particular turning problems.

16. Because of its depth and interior curvature, the finished bowl will look a bit different than the flat laminated assembly.

The appearance of the turning is pleasing. And there is a special satisfaction in having made a plain piece of wood into one with appeal and unlimited design possibilities.

White oak, and red oak with ebony veneer.
Dale L. Nish.

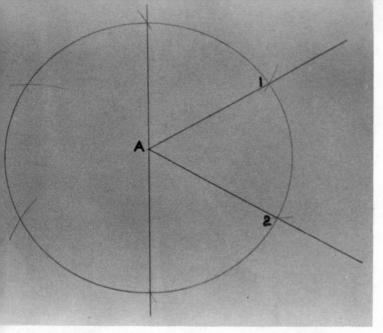

Segments and Solids

By combining segments with solid stock of various thicknesses and species, it is possible to produce turnings with many combinations of pattern and design. The following sequence is only one way to build up a bowl and must serve as a catalyst to start the turner experimenting with other variations.

In working with segments and solids, I have a few general guides. First, I try to keep the combinations of woods simple, avoiding high contrast in color or pattern. Second, I try to combine the woods in such a way that glue lines become part of the design, trying to eliminate the appearance that two pieces were laminated together just to produce a thicker piece of stock. Third, I use woods with relatively little figure, letting texture changes, such as end grain against flat grain, add interest to the piece. Fourth, when I do use high-contrast woods, I use them in small quantities, for accent lines or design breaks.

1.   Lay out a circle equal to the diameter of the bowl.

Divide the circle into six parts. These can be stepped off using the compass set at the same distance as was used to draw the circle.

Draw a center line through point A, and connect points 1 and 2 with point A. The angle enclosed by lines 1-A and 2-A will be 60 degrees.

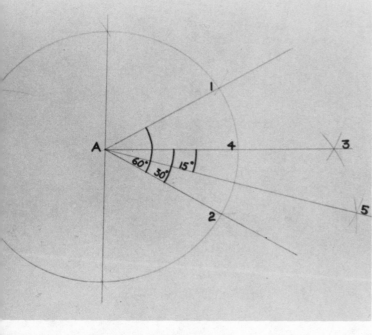

2.   Set the compass at points 1 and 2, making arcs that intersect at point 3. Connect points 3 and A. This divides the 60 degree area into two parts of 30 degrees each.

Using points 2 and 4, make arcs intersecting at point 5. Connect points 5 and A, dividing the 30 degree area into two parts of 15 degrees each.

3.   Using points 4 and 6, make arcs which intersect at point 7. Join point 7 to point A. This will divide the 15 degree area into two parts of 7½ degrees each.

Measure from point 4 towards point A a distance equal to the required length of the segments to be used in the turning. Put a mark on the line.

Set the compass leg at point A, and open the compass until it reaches the point on the line. Make an arc cutting lines 4-A and 6-A.

Shade in the enclosed area as shown. The shaded area will be equal to one segment. There will be twenty-four segments, each containing 15 degrees in each segmented ring. Each side of the segment will be cut at 7½ degrees.

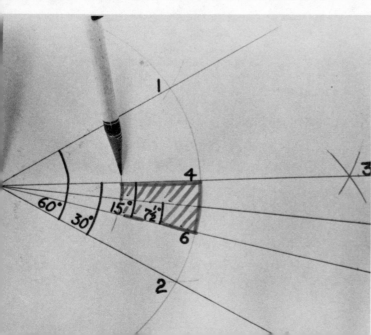

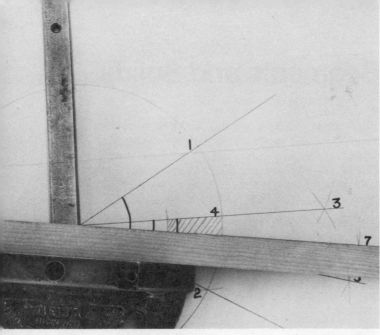

4.   Fasten a 3/4″ X 1½″ X 18″ facing strip to the miter gauge. The suggested measurements are not critical, but will work well.

Loosen the lock knob, and adjust the miter gauge to 7½ degrees. Check the setting by placing the miter gauge on the drawing. The gauge slide must line up with the center line, and the facing strip must line up with the 7½-degree line, A to point 7.

The marks on the miter-gauge scale are not accurate enough to be relied on when making this adjustment.

5.   Place the miter gauge in the slot on the saw, and adjust the blade to a height 1/8″ above the stock to be used for segments.

Start the saw and make a cut through the facing strip.

6.   Set the compass to a distance equal to the distance between points 4 and 6 (see Figure 3.)

Slide a stop block along the facing strip, and, using the compass as a gauge, position and clamp the block to the facing strip.

The measurement must be accurate.

7.   Using segment stock previously ripped to width, cut several segments.

Reverse the stock after each cut, to produce a 7½-degree cut on each side of the segment.

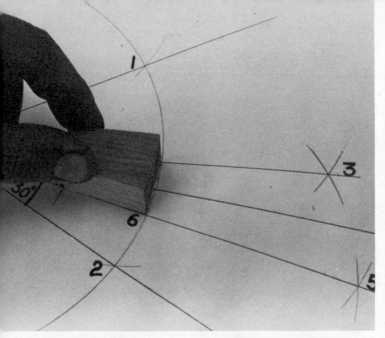

8. Take a segment and compare it to the shaded area on the pattern.

If it seems to fit, take four segments and fit them to a 30-degree space. This will show up any errors in the angle of the segments.

Make any necessary adjustments, and continue cutting segments until you have a few more than is required for the turning.

9. Check the segments to be sure the sides and faces are square.

10. Place the segments on a flat surface and check for squareness. The one on the left is not square. It must be sanded to the correct angle or rejected.

11. Set the sander table at a perfect 90 degrees to the sanding disc.

Lightly sand each side of each segment, being careful not to change the 7½-degree angle or remove too much stock.

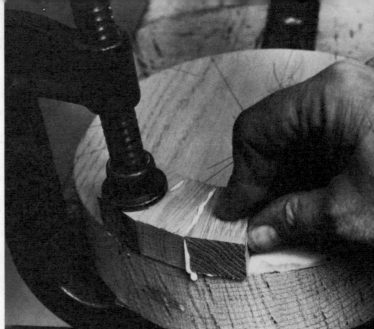

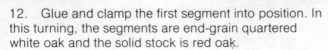

12.   Glue and clamp the first segment into position. In this turning, the segments are end-grain quartered white oak and the solid stock is red oak.

13.   Spread glue ahead of the blocks, and rub the segment into the glue.

14.   Applying pressure to the segment, rub it back and forth into position.

Be careful not to shift the other segments.

15.   As the ring nears completion, take three segments, hold them together, and check the fit with the opening.

If an adjustment needs to be made, make a small adjustment on each of the three segments, rather than all on one segment.

Using several segments will assure that the adjustments are small enough that they will not show.

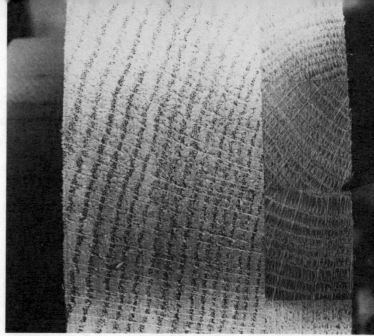

16.   Carefully fit the closing segment into position.

17.   Let the ring dry overnight, then true up the edge and face of the segmented ring.

18.   A close-up of a good fit. This is easy to do, if you are careful and pay attention to your work.

19.   An accent piece of ebony veneer has been glued in place, cured, and trued up on the lathe.

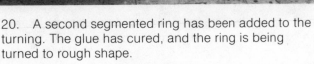

20.   A second segmented ring has been added to the turning. The glue has cured, and the ring is being turned to rough shape.

Be sure to turn the top edge true and flat.

21.   Another piece of solid stock has been band sawed to rough diameter and glued in place.

Note the matching of grain in the top solid piece with the grain in the solid base.

This helps give the appearance that the segmented rings and accent strip are inlaid into solid oak.

22.   The solid piece is turned to rough shape and the interior part removed.

It is easier to do this at this point, and the turned area will act as a guide for gluing the next segmented ring into place.

23.   Glue the next segmented ring into place.

Excellent joinery is critical here, as the ring will form the top edge of the turning and will be visible from the sides as well as from the top.

24.   Complete the rough turning of the exterior of the container. I use a roundnose to bring areas into shape.

25.   The final finish cut can be made with a sharp gouge. Take a light even cut, with the gouge in shearing position.

26.   Finish the turning with 60, 80, 100, 150 and 180 or 220 grit paper.

Be sure that each grit has removed all the scratches left from the previous grit before changing grit sizes. Changing to a finer grit too quickly will prolong the sanding process.

27.   Use a sharp roundnose chisel and turn out the interior of the container.

The lip around the top will emphasize the segmented pattern and will serve to hold the lid in place.

28. Turn a lid to fit the container.

For this turning, quartered white oak is used to complement the end-grain quartered white oak used in the segmented rings.

29. The lid should complement the shape of the container and should be decorative and functional.

Sand completely, and apply an oil finish.

30. Several coats of oil are applied to the container. Each coat is allowed to penetrate into the wood and then is wiped dry with the container spinning on the lathe.

31.   Place the faceplate assembly on a support block, and separate the wooden disc from the base of the container.

The block should be thick enough to allow the turning to clear the band saw table by about 1/8''.

Hold the turning and faceplate assembly securely to prevent the saw blade from grabbing the piece and spinning it off the block, perhaps ruining the turning and injuring the operator.

32.   The finished turning. Note in the lid the prominent figure produced from the ray pattern in the quartered white oak.

Walnut and maple, 15" high. Dale L. Nish.

Built-up Mosaic Turnings

Built-up turnings can be assembled in many different ways, including segmented rings, staved pieces, and flat laminations. The method presented in this unit was inspired by native basketry designs. It was my intent to construct a turning that looked as if it had been constructed from a solid block of wood with the pattern inlaid rather than from several different blocks. The viewer must determine how successful I have been. But more important, I hope this process will encourage others to experiment and develop turnings that they find satisfying.

With this type of turning, planning and designing is very important. A full-size drawing must be completed and each section clearly defined. Refine the shape until it is appealing to you and has the appearance you require. If you have a problem determining shape, you will find that books showing works produced on the potter's wheel are a good source of shapes and sizes. Another source is catalogs showing crystal or glass products. Study examples of form and shape, then design a turning that you feel good about.

Design the turning full size. A large sheet of graph paper makes a good choice, because it can also be used to lay out the mosaic pattern.

Mark break lines as well as interior shape and wall thicknesses.

Try to plan each part of the turning so that the areas with no design can be turned from a solid block of wood.

It is also helpful if all the solid parts can be cut from the same block of wood. This helps create the illusion that the turning has an inlaid design, particularly if care is taken to glue up the turning in a way that takes maximum advantage of the figure and color in the solid stock.

1.   Mount the rough blank on the lathe, and turn the exterior to the required shape.

A gouge works well on a surface such as this.

2.   Bore a depth hole into the base piece, stopping about 3/4″ from the bottom.

3.   Turn the inside of the base to rough shape.

The photo shows a modified square-nose being used to remove 3/8″ sections in one pass.

4. The cleanup tool is the gouge.

Take a light cut, and keep the gouge sharp.

Leave a 5/8″ to 3/4″ wall thickness.

5. Face the top edge, and check to be sure that it is true and flat.

6. Draw a circle equal to the diameter of the top of the base piece.

Use a compass and divide the circumference into equal sections.

For this turning, I decided to use forty-eight sections for each ring of mosaic pieces.

This gives an angle of 3 ¾ degrees for each side of each mosaic piece.

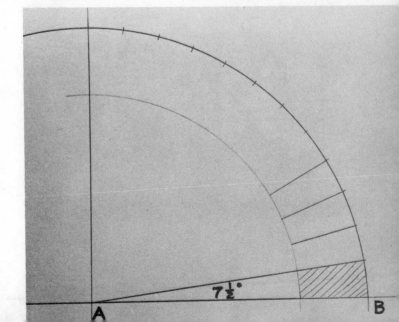

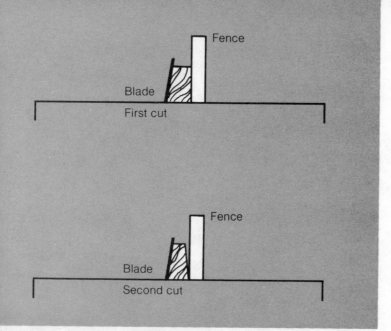

Fence

Blade

First cut

Fence

Blade

Second cut

7.   Select a piece of stock that is flat and true and at least 3/4'' thick. The number of pieces of stock needed will vary with each pattern, but be sure to cut enough.

If several colors of wood are used, be sure to cut all the pieces at the same saw setting.

Tilt the saw blade to the required angle, and set the fence to the required width.

Make a ripping cut, then turn the stock over and make another cut. The strips then will be beveled to the correct angle, in this case 3 ¾ degrees.

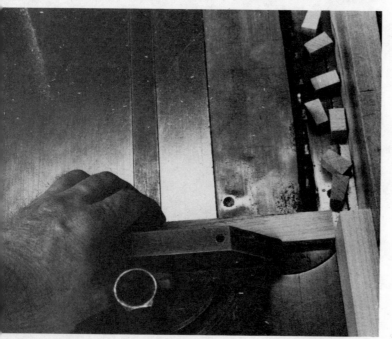

8.   Clamp a clearance block to the fence, and adjust the block and fence to the required distance from the blade.

The distance is determined by the height of the mosaic piece.

Use a miter gauge and cut the required number of pieces, plus a few extra.

Group the pieces according to color, and place each group in an individual container for future use.

9.   Find a starting point, and glue the mosaic pieces around the top of the base.

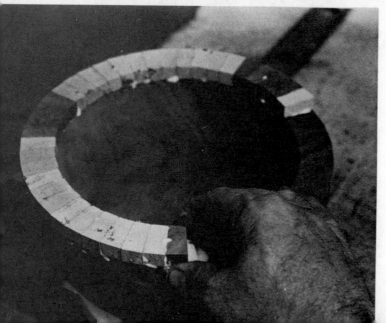

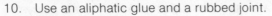

10.   Use an aliphatic glue and a rubbed joint.

Force the pieces together firmly, but be careful not to loosen the adjoining piece.

Use plenty of glue; you are working with end-grain.

11.   Periodically check the angle of the piece to be sure the alignment with the center of the turning is correct.

Small errors add up. Consequently, it may be necessary to change the angle of a piece to correct alignment problems.

If close attention is paid to the cutting angle, adjustments will be few.

12.   The closing piece must fit well. Check the fit carefully before applying glue and setting the piece in place.

13.   Small adjustments in size or angle can easily be made on a disc sander.

Be sure the table is at right angles to the disc.

14.   Place glue on the closing piece, as well as on the sides of the neighboring pieces.

Force the closing piece into the space.

Let set for several hours, or overnight.

15.   After the glue has set, use a sharp roundnose to true up the surface.

Do not change the diameter of the turning. That is, do not cut below the surface of the original piece.

16.   True up the top of the mosaic ring.

Remove as little stock as possible.

Take light cuts, use a sharp tool, and check frequently.

Don't true up the inside of the ring; the inside part acts as a guide for setting the next row.

17.   Using a straightedge, check to be sure the ring surface is true and flat.

If necessary, take a light cut to make the adjustments required.

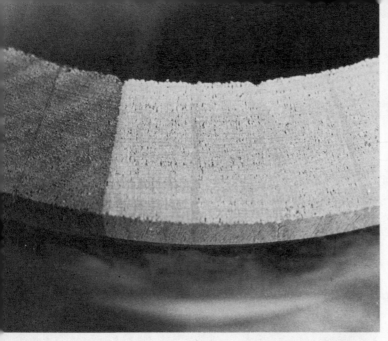

18. This is a close-up of a properly fit and glued ring of mosaic pieces.

19. This shows several mosaic pieces set in place and the surfaces trued up.

Note the close fit. Some glue lines are nearly invisible.

20. A photo of poorly fit pieces.

Note the gaps between the pieces, as well as the pieces being out of square.

This was caused by lack of attention to detail, by using *one* piece that was not square.

21. Note the large gap caused by not forcing the piece down against the ring.

Try to avoid these common errors.

22.   The turning is built up with a series of mosaic rings.

23.   Each ring has the face and top trued up before the next ring is added.

Carefully check the design to prevent errors in the pattern. It is difficult to correct an error, particularly if several rings are added before the error is discovered.

Check twice—glue once.

24.   As each ring is closed, problems may develop. Sometimes it is necessary to sand two or more pieces to ensure a proper fit.

A good fit is always top priority, because poor-fitting joints are usually weak joints.

25.   The top ring is in place, and the design is complete. The last of 384 mosaic pieces has been glued in place.

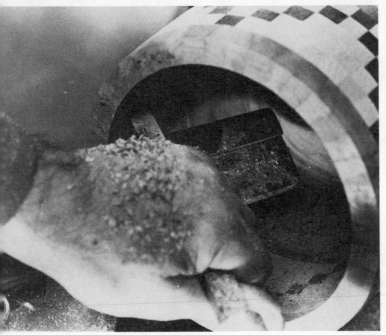

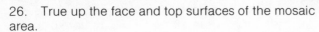

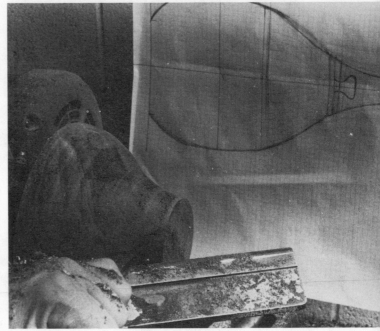

26. True up the face and top surfaces of the mosaic area.

Try to turn the exterior surface to final shape.

27. Shape the interior surfaces, leaving a wall thickness of 1/2'' to 5/8''.

Proceed carefully, particularly at the beginning, due to the irregular interior surface left from gluing up the mosaic pattern.

28. Rough sand the interior surface.

It is not necessary to sand the interior to a high-quality surface; the interior will not show after the turning is complete.

29. Block out the part to be fastened to the mosaic area.

Turn the exterior to rough shape, and bring the top part into round.

Face the top part true and flat.

The stock has been fastened to a screw-center faceplate.

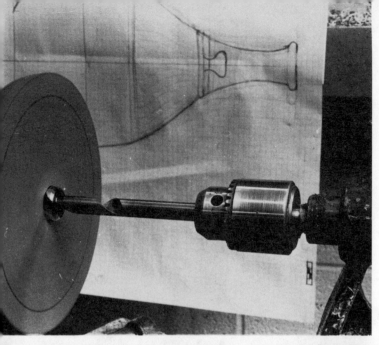

30. Bore a hole through the piece.

The piece is reversed and held with a three-jaw chuck or with a faceplate.

31. Shape the interior of the piece until a required wall thickness has been reached.

The wall should be 1/2'' to 5/8'' at the base, tapering to 3/8'' to 1/2'' at the top.

Properly used, a gouge works well for his operation.

32. Check the contact surfaces for a tight fit.

This can best be achieved by leaving the interior of the joint slightly open, causing a very close fit at the exterior surface.

Check for color and figure alignment with the solid stock below the mosaic area.

Get the best effect possible, then glue into place.

Remember—the mosaic should appear to be set into the wood rather than looking as though it has been placed between two separate pieces.

Use a disc to distribute clamp pressure.

Do not use excessive pressure.

33. A small mosaic ring is glued to the top of the solid piece.

34. Use a disc and light pressure to help control vibration problems.

Turn the ring until it blends into the solid piece.

35. Smooth the interior of the ring, and blend it into the lower neck.

A sharp skew, held as shown, does a good job with this operation.

36.   The top part of the neck is roughed out.

Bore a hole through the neck.

The hole must be the same size as the smallest inside diameter of the neck.

Reverse the ends of the neck (I use a three-jaw chuck) and turn the inside base of the neck to a diameter equal to the interior diameter of the mosaic ring.

Blend the large opening into the smaller part of the neck.

Face the base of the neck true and flat.

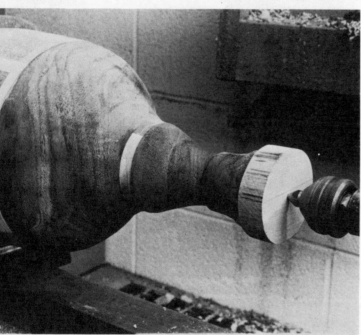

37.   Glue the neck in place.

Using the lathe as a clamp, let the assembly dry for thirty minutes.

Now remove the complete turning from the lathe and let the glue dry overnight.

38.   Place the turning on the lathe, and blend the surface areas until the shape is the same as the pattern.

It is good practice to keep the tailstock in place, with the dead center and disc exerting light pressure on the top. This helps control vibration problems (the total length of the turning is now fifteen inches).

Do not remove too much stock, as the turning will be weakened.

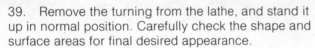

39. Remove the turning from the lathe, and stand it up in normal position. Carefully check the shape and surface areas for final desired appearance.

40. Place the turning on the lathe and make the final cuts.

Here a gouge is used to make final cleanup cuts on the base.

If you are more comfortable with a roundnose, sharpen it and take a light cut.

41. The last cut is blending the opening of the neck into the hole bored with the multispur bit.

A sharp skew chisel used as shown works well for this job.

Vibration is a problem, so take a light, steady cut.

42. Finish the turning with the abrasive papers you normally use. I start with 60 grit, then go to 80, 100, 150 and 220.

After sanding with 220, select a used piece of 150 and sand with the grain and with the turning stopped. This will remove any circular sanding marks.

43.   With the parting tool, partially separate the turning from the wooden disc on the faceplate.

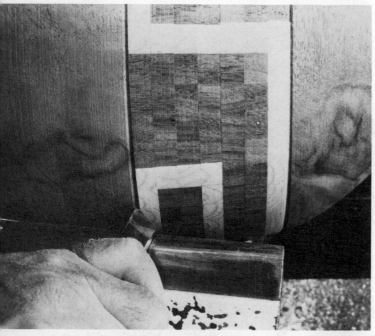

44.   This operation is optional.

Sharpen the skew, and make a V-joint where the mosaic design is glued to the solid stock. These cuts are shallow, and they emphasize the design.

Do the same thing on the neck where the inlay ring meets the other parts.

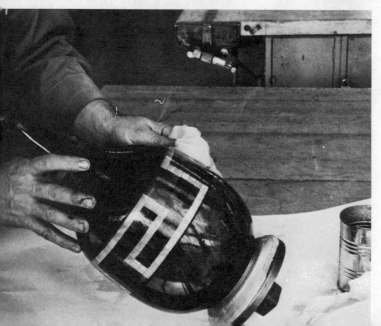

45.   One way to finish the turning is to apply an oil finish. Many good ones are available from paint stores. This piece could also be finished with lacquer or other surface finishes, but I feel that a glossy surface would detract from the natural appearance of the turning.

After completely finishing the turning, use a hand saw or band saw to separate the turning from the faceplate.

Sand the base true and flat.

Walnut with oak branches. Dale L. Nish.

Inlay with Oak Branches

Many inlays have been used, such as dowels, square pegs, triangular pieces, and random blocks. Most of these patterns are symmetrical in shape and design. But wood is a natural material, and a less formal inlay method can be developed using oak roots or branches. In my experience, there is little difference between the cross-sectional appearances of a branch and a root. In fact, a root is basically an underground branch. Nevertheless, I prefer working with branches because usually they are straighter and easier to acquire than roots. Cut the branches and let them dry thoroughly before using them for inlay work. I am sure branches from other species could be used for inlay, but oak branches are particularly attractive because they have such prominent medullary rays.

1.   A group of oak branches, showing a few of the typical patterns that appear in sectional cuts. Each piece is different in color, ray pattern, or both.

2.   A band saw simplifies the task of cutting the branches into short, straight lengths.

Try for cuttings six to ten inches in length.

3.   An armful of oak branches that have been dried and cut to working lengths.

4.   Mount the piece between centers and turn it to rough size. A few bark patches will be acceptable. They can be removed when the piece is further turned to the desired size.

5.   A bundle of rough-turned oak branches, ready for inlay work.

Note the pattern variation in the ends of the pieces—a wonderful example of nature's work, as different as snowflakes.

6.   This sequence will show an inlay method for a dried-flower vase.

End trim the limb until all checks are removed.

Walnut and other species of limb wood, thoroughly dried, work well for these types of turnings.

7.   Band saw the blank to a rough cylinder.

8.   Mount the cylinder between centers, and turn to rough shape.

A gouge works well for this operation.

The cuts will be clean and smooth, because end-grain is only on the top and bottom of the cylinder.

9.   Stop the lathe occasionally, and examine the piece for shape and defects in the wood.

Defects may have an effect in determining the final shape of the piece.

10.   After the turning has been turned to basically the finished shape, mark a 1/8" to 1/4" line at approximately where you want to drill the inlay holes.

11.   Multispur bits work very well and are available in many sizes. They are my choice for this operation, because if they are properly sharpened and securely held, they cut fast and clean.

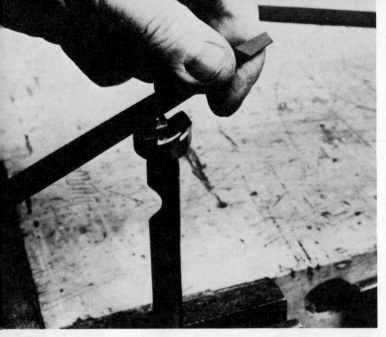

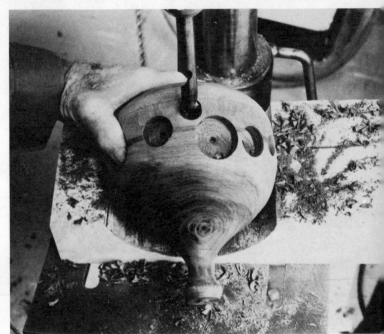

12.   If necessary, touch up the bits before using them. A clean, smooth cut is essential if a top-quality inlay is desired.

13.   A holding block is important for accurate and safe work.

Take a scrap block 2½'' or 3'' thick by about 6'' wide and at least as long as the width of the drill-press table.

Mark and use the band saw to cut an arc in the block. The radius must be the same as the largest radius of the turning piece into which the holes will be bored.

Install a multispur bit, and center the block under the bit.

14.   Place the turning in the holding block, lower the bit, and check to be sure the bit will drill a hole that, if drilled deep enough, would penetrate to the center point of the turning.

Adjust the table to left or right if necessary, and raise or lower the neck of the turning to properly position the piece.

15.   Drill a series of holes around the circumference of the piece.

Drill the largest holes first, then the next largest, and so on, down to the smallest hole.

Do not allow the holes to touch one another.

Drill the holes about 1/2'' deep.

This vase is being drilled for an informal pattern.

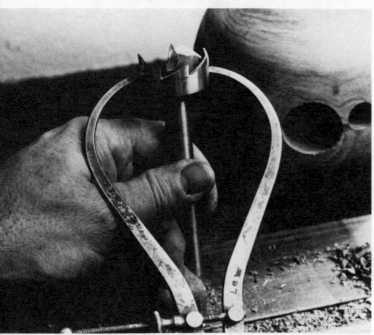

16. Place a rough-turned dowel on the lathe. Here I am using a three-jaw chuck, which works well for this operation. However, if the dowel were glue-chucked into a wooden disc on a faceplate, that would work just as well.

17. To establish the rough diameter of the plug, use calipers and set them using the bit as a gauge.

18. Establish the parting line about 5/8″ in from the end of the dowel.

Using the parting tool, cut into the right end of the dowel until the required diameter is reached.

19. Check the rough diameter with calipers, and make the final depth cut.

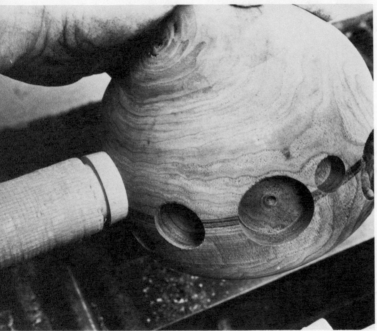

20.   Turn the plug to the required finished diameter.

Here a skew chisel and a light, shearing cut is used.

Slightly taper the plug from the parting cut to the end.

21.   Use the hole in the turning as the final check.

A good fit is one in which the plug penetrates about three-quarters of the way into the hole before firm resistance is felt.

Continue with light, shearing cuts until the correct size is reached.

Use as many different dowels as you can, to give variety to the plugs.

22.   As each plug is cut, number it and number the hole.

Leave the loosely fit plug in the hole until all the plugs have been cut and fit.

23.   Apply glue in the hole and to the plug.

Do not trap a pocket of glue in the hole.

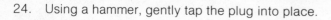

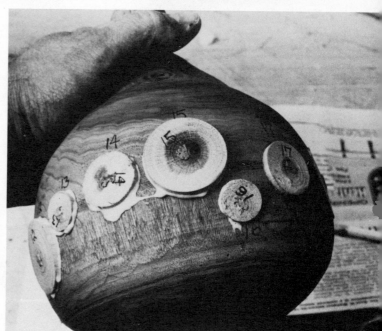

24. Using a hammer, gently tap the plug into place.

25. If a plug is a little tight, use a vise to force it into place.

It is not necessary to leave the turning in the vise for more than a minute or so. Once the air trapped in the hole has had a chance to move out through the wood fibers, friction will hold the plug in place.

26. A dowel or the end of a pencil makes a good tool for spreading the glue uniformly around the hole.

Glue in one plug at a time.

27. Once the plugs have been glued in place, they should be allowed to dry completely before they are turned off.

Tight-fitting plugs can be turned after the glue has been drying for an hour or so, but is best to let the glue dry overnight.

28. Place the turning between centers, and turn off the plugs until the surface is clean and smooth.

Do not turn deeper than just flush with the existing surface of the vase.

A sharp gouge does a good job, but a sharp roundnose could be used as well.

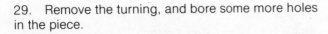

29. Remove the turning, and bore some more holes in the piece.

As before, do not let the holes touch each other. But the holes can overlap existing plugs if this is desired.

I try to get an informal design, using several different sizes of holes, and informal spacing.

In this turning, the plugs will eventually form a continuous ring around the turning but will not be in any particular alignment.

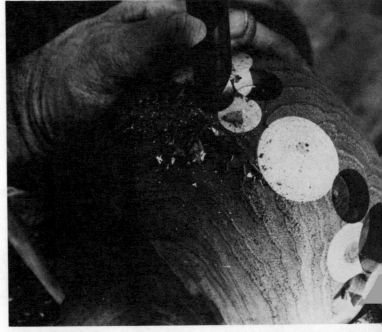

30. Make the final cleanup and shaping cuts using a sharp gouge or roundnose chisel.

Do not remove more wood than necessary to give the final shape.

Certainly do not turn through the plugs, as the piece will be ruined.

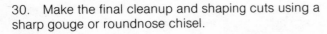

114

31. A sharp roundnose is being used for the final shaping of the neck.

32. Using a skew in flat position, shape the inside of the top as much as you can.

Be careful not to cut deep enough to remove the center part. If you do, the piece will fly off the lathe.

33. This is a critical operation, and a mistake can ruin a very nice turning.

Get someone to help, if you can. The piece must not be allowed to turn or move.

Start out with a small bit, such as 3/16'' or 1/4'', and bore a pilot hole through the neck and down into the body of the piece.

Use several bits, each a little larger than the one before, gradually enlarging the hole to the required size.

Do not make the wall neck too thin. If you do, the bit may come through the side, or the neck may twist or break off.

34. Apply the finish as you desire. I prefer several coats of Danish oil or Tung oil.

Walnut with oak branches. Dale L. Nish.

Decorative Pegging with Oak-Branch Pegs

1. Fasten a wooden disc to the face and bore a 1/4″ hole through the disc.

If this is done on the lathe, the hole will be perfectly centered.

Later this hole will contain a 1/4″ dowel that will be used to center the turning on the faceplate.

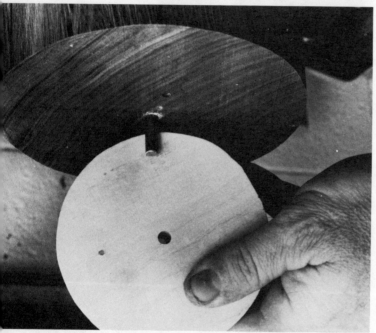

2. A matching 1/4″ hole, approximately 1/2″ to 3/4″ deep is drilled in the true and flat base of the rough-sawed block.

The hole in the base of the block is used for centering the block on the indexing unit, as well as for centering the block on the faceplate.

3. Place a 1/4″ X 1½″ steel pin in the hole in the : block.

Moisten the base of the block. The damp base of the block will be pressed against the faceplate, and the friction will allow the block to be rough turned.

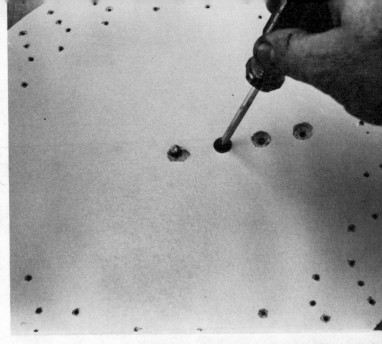

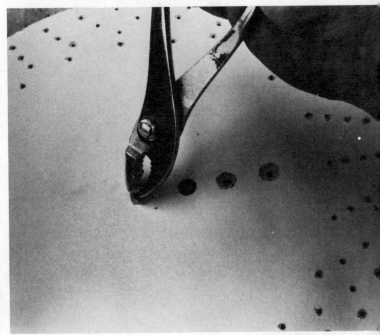

4. The steel pin in the base of the block is inserted into the hole in the wooden faceplate. With the ball-bearing center in place, exert firm pressure, holding the block tight against the faceplate.

5. Turn the block to rough shape.

Turn a shoulder at the point where you want to insert the pegs. The shoulder should be deep enough to allow the drill bit to bore on a flat surface, with the holes 1/8″ or more away from the surface of the turning.

6. Remove the turning from the lathe, and turn it upside down.

The pin in the base of the turning is inserted into the center hole in the indexing wheel.

Drive a screw through the indexing wheel and into the base of the turning.

7. Pull the pin out of the base of the turning.

Be careful not to change the position of the turning on the index wheel.

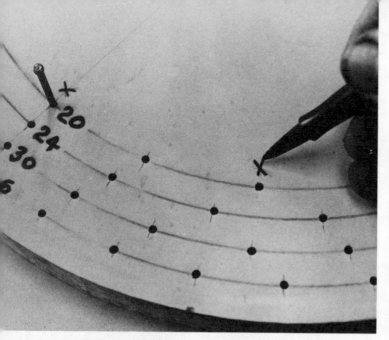

8.   Turn the indexing wheel over, and place the wheel and turning onto the pin in the indexing base.

Mark the desired number of holes on the indexing wheel.

For this turning, every other hole on the twenty-hole circle will be used. This will give ten holes in the turning, or one every 36 degrees.

9.   With the indexing pin in the "Start" hole, bore a hole to the desired depth.

In this sequence the holes are 5/8" in diameter and 1¼" deep. This will allow the pegs to be turned off on one side, giving an elliptical appearance in the turning.

10.   After each hole is bored, pull the indexing pin, rotate the wheel to the next desired point, insert the indexing pin into the base hole, and bore a hole.

Continue the process until all the holes have been bored.

11.   A piece of oak branch is turned to rough size between centers on the lathe.

Calipers are set slightly over the desired diameter, and diameters are established using the calipers and parting tool.

12.   The peg is turned to final diameter using a skew chisel and a shearing cut.

The diameter must be accurate and the same all the way along.

One way to make a final check is to bore a hole of the required size in a scrap block, and slide the block over the turned peg. This will easily show any problems with peg size.

13.   Cut the peg to required length, and set the peg in the hole.

The holes may vary in size slightly, so I try to find the best-fitting hole for each peg.

14.   Place a little glue in the hole, and wipe it all around the inside of the hole.

A piece of dowel rod or a pencil works well for this job.

15.   Insert the peg in the hole, and pull it into place using a clamp or the bench vise.

Pressure needs to be steady and constant, to allow air trapped in the hole to escape through the hole or the wood fibers.

After a minute or two, the clamp can be removed and the next peg installed.

16.   Replace the 1/4'' steel pin in the base of the turning with a piece of 1/4'' dowel.

Glue the wooden disc to the base of the turning.

The dowel will keep the two pieces in alignment and will not interfere with the turning operation if a tool accidentally cuts into it.

Place the faceplate and turning on the lathe, and use the tailstock as a clamp.

Allow to dry overnight.

Use a gouge or roundnose to rough out the shape of the container.

Do not turn so deep or far down the piece that the bottom ends of the pegs are exposed. Be sure to allow for the stock that will be removed during the sanding process.

17.   Bore a hole to the bottom of the container. I usually leave the bottom 1/2'' to 3/4'' thick.

18.   Turn the interior of the container to a wall thickness of 1/4''.

On the top edge, turn a lip to receive the lid.

A roundnose works well on the interior of the container as well as for shaping the top edge.

121

19. Partially separate the container from the wooden disc.

This will allow easier and complete sanding of the exposed areas of the container.

20. Select a piece of stock suitable for the lid and glue it to a wooden disc.

Fasten the unit to a faceplate small enough to fit inside the container.

21. A hole has been bored into the lid.

An oak branch has been turned to fit the hole and has been glued in place.

This branch will become the knob on the lid.

22.   Turn the lid to the desired shape and fit.

This shows a lid that will set down into the container.

23.   Place the faceplate and lid in the opening in the container.

Check for fit, and make any necessary adjustments in shape or size.

Do not get the lid too small.

Sand the lid, then separate the lid from the faceplate.

Walnut with oak branches. Dale L. Nish.

Decorative Pegging— Offset Rows

1.   Follow the series of steps shown in Figures 1–4 under "Decorative Pegging with Oak-Branch Pegs."

Turn the block to rough shape.

Turn a shoulder at the point where the pegs will be inserted. The shoulder must be deep enough to allow for two rows of holes. The amount the rows will be offset will be determined by the design and final shape of the turning.

2.   Mount the roughed-out turning on the indexing wheel (see Figures 6–8 under "Decorative Pegging with Oak-Branch Pegs").

Position the turning, and bore the outside row of holes. In this operation the holes are 1/2" X 1½" deep.

The pegs will have an elliptical appearance when the turning is completed.

3.   Position the turning for boring the second row of holes. In this operation these holes are 1/2" X 1". The pegs can be shorter, as only the tops of them will show.

These holes could be larger or smaller, and spacing could be changed for different appearances.

The design options are practically unlimited.

4. Glue and clamp the oak-branch pegs in the holes.

Let the glue cure overnight.

5. Turn the base of the turning to final shape.

Notice the unique patterns produced by the elliptical shapes.

6. Bore a depth hole.

From this point, the turning could be made into a bowl, a covered container, or a vase.

7.   The turning is partially hollowed out, and the top of the opening is tapered in.

An oak branch is turned to fit the opening and is glued into place.

The lathe is used as a clamp, and the turning is left overnight to allow the glue to cure.

8.   Turn the vase to final shape.

Note that the inside top of the vase has been shaped with the lathe center still in place. This reduces vibration during the turning of the piece.

9.   The neck of the vase has been bored through, using a multispur bit, while the vase was still on the lathe.

The top opening was blended into the hole, using a small roundnose chisel.

The vase has been completely sanded and an oil finish applied.

This is just one of many possibilities using the pegging technique.

Buckeye burl. 6″ X 10″ Hap Sakwa.

Weed Pots

1.   Weed pots can be turned from wood pieces that otherwise would be burned or discarded. I have used dead limb wood, weathered posts, burls, roots, branches, and assorted blocks.

Because these pots typically are used for displaying dried weeds or flowers, I try to leave natural surfaces—with a polished top for an interesting contrast.

2.   Lay out the required diameter. This piece of Indian rosewood will have portions of the rough block left on one side of the finished turning. The layout should be on the top of the block.

3.   Machine the bottom of the block flat and true.

Band saw the block to rough shape.

4. Find the center point on the bottom of the block, and drill a pilot hole for the screw-center faceplate.

5. Select a screw-center faceplate, and install it on the lathe. It is best to have the faceplate smaller than the finished base of the weed pot, but a larger one can be used.

Fasten the stock to the faceplate.

Use a chuck mounted in the tailstock, and drill a hole the desired diameter and to the necessary depth. The hole diameter should be the same as the diameter of the rod you will use.

6. I had a machinist make several rods about seven inches long, with small diameters of 1/4", 3/8", and 1/2". The heavy base of the rod is about 2½" long and is tapered to fit into a ball-bearing center. The required rod is placed in a hole drilled into the center of the pot and is used to apply pressure against the stock and faceplate. The rod also stabilizes long necks and wood that is weak or contains defects. It also helps eliminate vibration during the turning of the pot.

7. Using a chuck mounted in the tailstock, drill a hole of the desired diameter to the necessary depth.

Remove the center from the ball-bearing center, and install the rod.

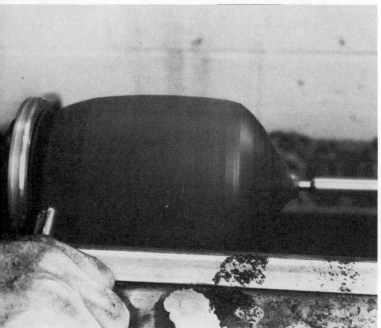

8. Move the tailstock into position, and insert the rod into the turning until it reaches the bottom.

Apply medium pressure to the rod. This will help secure the block to the faceplate and will cut down vibration during the shaping of the piece.

9. Rough shape the turning. If the faceplate is larger than the base of the turning, leave a small disc. This will be removed later.

A shearing cut leaves a fine surface.

10. The final shaping, particularly around the neck, can be done with a newly sharpened roundnose.

Take light cuts, blending the shape to its final form.

11. Remove the unit from the lathe, and take a close look at the shape. I like to see the turning in its normal position. This allows one to better evaluate the form and to determine if further shaping is necessary.

12.   Using a parting tool, partially separate the base from the faceplate.

Sand the turning.

Note the pleasing contrast between the rough area and the sanded surfaces.

Weed Pots (Black-Locust Post)

1.   These weed pots were turned from a black-locust post that had weathered to a silver gray surface. The wood was sound, with few radial checks.

2.   Mount the block on a screw center, and bore the center hole.

3. Turn the top to the desired shape.

Use a sharp gouge with a shearing cut. When properly used, the gouge will cut smooth enough that the surface will not require sanding.

4. Note the contrast between the smooth surface and simple form and the weathered exterior of the block. Also, the different widths of the growth rings add interest to the texture and appearance of the top. Other shapes and possibilities are almost unlimited.

5. I try to keep the form of the pot simple, depending on the contrasting textures and varied sizes to give the pots interest and compatibility for groupings.

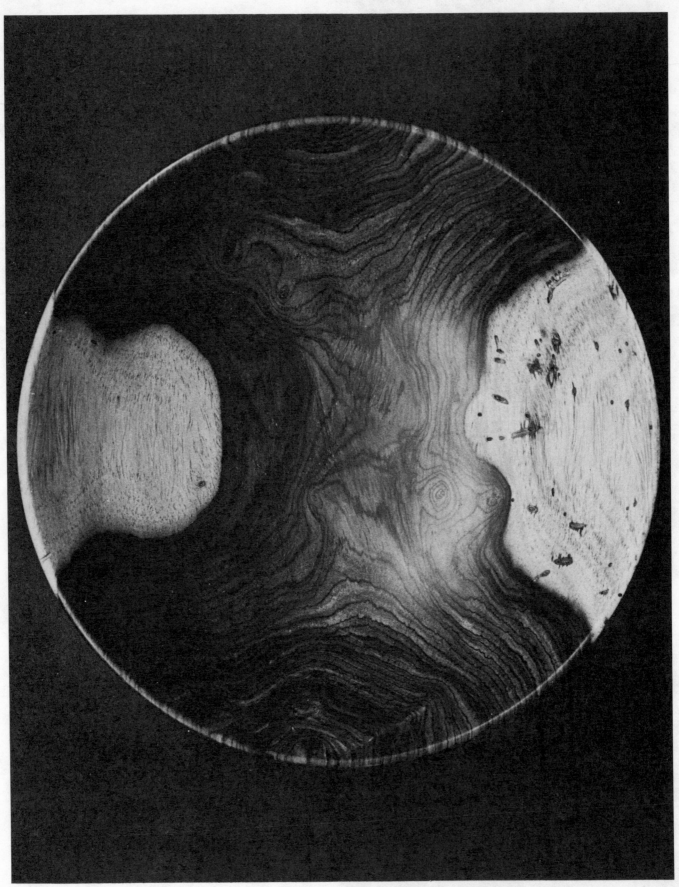

Cocobolo. Al Stirt. *Photo by Roy Gifford.*

Plates (Turned with a Screw Center and a Three-Jaw Chuck)

1. Cut out a wooden disc the desired diameter and approximately one inch thick.

A good diameter is from eleven to twelve inches.

Drill a pilot hole for the screw center, and screw the disc onto the faceplate. Use a shim piece if necessary.

The hole should not be more than 1/2″ to 5/8″ deep. Otherwise, when the hole has been turned out, there is not enough wood left to turn a base on the plate.

2. Move the tailstock into position, and advance the ball-bearing center until it applies firm pressure against the stock.

3. True up the edge of the stock, and mark the base of the plate.

An eleven- to twelve-inch plate requires a base six to seven inches in diameter. A general rule is that the base should be a little more than one-half the diameter of the plate.

4. Turn the outside of the plate shape.

A sharp gouge or roundnose is the best choice for this operation.

The surface should be smooth, with a gradual transition from edge to surface to base.

5. Once the base area has been established, a straight or slightly inward-beveled shoulder must be turned to a depth of approximately 1/4''. This is to allow an area for the three-jaw chuck to grip securely.

6. Form the inner area of the base, leaving a flat rim about 5/8'' to 3/4'' in width. Later this rim will be reduced to 3/8'' to 1/2'' in width, as the base is turned to final shape.

7. Using a square-nose, turn the center of the base flat and true.

8. Sand the bottom of the plate to a finished surface. Use the usual grit sequence, finishing with 220 paper.

9. Install the three-jaw chuck on the headstock spindle.

Secure the base of the plate in the jaws of the chuck. Use medium pressure.

Be sure the plate is flat against each of the three jaws.

10. Exerting too much pressure may break a piece from the base of the plate.

If this happens, glue the piece back, rotate the plate to another position, and tighten the chuck.

11. Shape the interior of the plate.

It is very important to shape the plate to final wall thickness as the turning proceeds from the edge to the center of the plate.

Turn a small area at a time, usually 1'' to 1½''. Take this area down to final shape and thickness before removing stock from the rest of the inside of the plate. Working from the outside toward the center and following the instructions practically eliminates vibration because you are always working against thick wood.

12. The final cuts will leave a small post directly under the ball-bearing center.

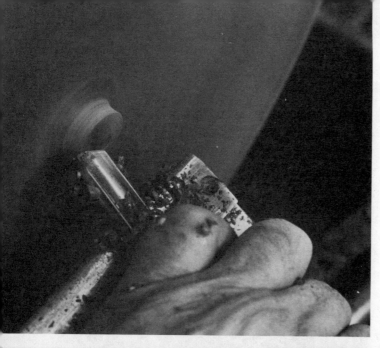

13. Move the tailstock out of the way, and carefully turn off the post.

14. Check the center of the plate for flatness, or at least to show a gradual slope and pleasing shape.

If necessary, make fine shearing cuts to achieve the desired shape.

The tools must be sharp and the cuts light, or vibration will become a major problem.

Completely sand the interior of the plate.

Remove the plate and three-jaw chuck from the lathe.

15. Cut out a plywood disc about two inches larger than the diameter of the plate.

Fasten the disc to a standard faceplate, and install the unit on the lathe.

Mark the plate diameter on the disc.

16.   Turn the surface of the disc to the shape of the interior of the plate.

The plate should fit snugly inside the rim of the disc.

The center area of the disc must be in contact with and support the center of the plate.

17.   Bore a 3/4″ hole in the center of the disc.

This hole is to allow the plate to be pushed off the disc once the outside of the plate is completed.

18.   Fit the plate into the recessed area of the disc.

A snug fit is best, but if the plate is a little loose, center the plate in the area.

19. Move the tailstock into place, and advance the ball-bearing center until it is in firm contact with the base.

Using a small, sharp roundnose chisel, blend the flat edge of the rim until it produces a satisfactory base for the plate.

20. Sand the newly turned area, and clean up any other areas that need touching up.

21. Apply the desired finish. Oil is my preference. The finish can be easily renewed and will actually improve with each application.

Walnut and spalted oak. Del Stubbs.

Inlaid Covered Boxes

1.   Covered boxes with inlaid lids offer an opportunity for the craftsman to create unique turnings that display exceptional pieces of wood as inlays in the lid. Such boxes intrigue the turner because they afford limitless opportunities in shapes, species of wood, and size. This sequence is based on techniques demonstrated by Del Stubbs of Chico, California, a very talented woodturner.

2.   Select a piece of wood large enough for the complete box, plus an extra 1/2'' or more in height (to allow for the parting off of the lid and the inner lip of the box).

The best way to lay out the box is to have the wood grain running vertically. This will give the box maximum freedom from warping.

True up the base of the block. A disc sander works well, but other methods can be used.

3.   Band saw the block to shape, and glue a wooden disc to the base of the piece.

The wooden disc will allow the block to be mounted to the faceplate without having screws or the screw center entering the block.

Glue directly to the block, as the joint must be secure, and the box will be separated from the disc with the use of a parting tool.

4.   In this photo, the disc is fastened to a screw-center faceplate.

The pen mark is used as a registration point.

If the turning is removed and remounted later, the point allows the disc to be placed in the exact position in which the original turning was done. This is critical for accurate work.

5.   Turn the box to its rough shape.

A gouge or sharp roundnose tool will do a good job.

Keep in mind that the final shape of the box will be about 1/2'' less in height than the rough turning.

6.   Lay out and mark the lip and lid of the box.

The distance between the lines should be 1/2'' to 5/8''. At least 1/8'' of the wood will be lost to the parting tool during removal of the lid.

7.   Use a sharp parting tool, and make a groove 1/4'' deep and 1/2'' to 5/8'' wide.

Be sure the sides of the groove are cut clean and true.

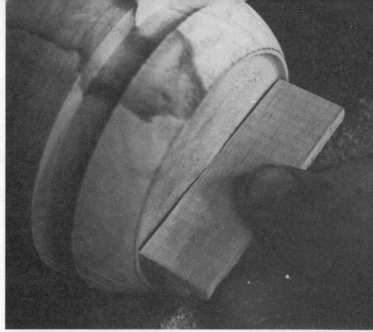

8. Turn the top of the box to the shape it will have when the inlay is complete.

At this point the shape is for design purposes only, but it is good to be able to see the final shape of the box.

Make any necessary changes in size or shape.

9. Use a sharp square-nose chisel, and cut the recess for the inlay piece.

10. Use a straightedge to check the recess bottom to be sure it is flat and true.

This recess is high in the center. More wood must be removed.

11. This recess is true and flat—ready to receive the inlay.

The wall of the recess should have a slight inward taper. I feel this allows the inlay to be fit into the recess more easily.

Never allow the recess walls to taper outward. Such a condition would make a good fit impossible.

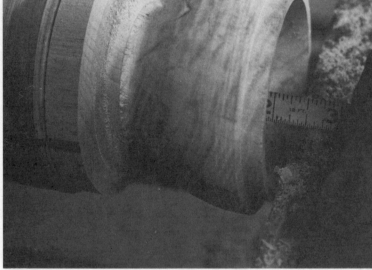

12.   Part the lid from the main body of the box.

Use a sharp tool, and slightly enlarge the width of the cut as you progress toward the center. Enlarging the cut will help prevent the parting tool from grabbing, binding, or overheating.

13.   Stop the lathe, and twist the lid from the main part of the box when there is only a small piece of wood (1/4″ or less) holding the lid in place.

With experience and practice, the lid can be separated from the box while the lathe is running at slow speed, one hand grasping the lid and the other hand holding and controlling the parting tool.

14.   Shape the interior of the box. A sharp roundnose works well if the inside of the bottom is rounded.

If the bottom is flat, a sharp square-nose is the tool to use.

15.   Measure the depth of the box. Leave about 1/4″ in the bottom.

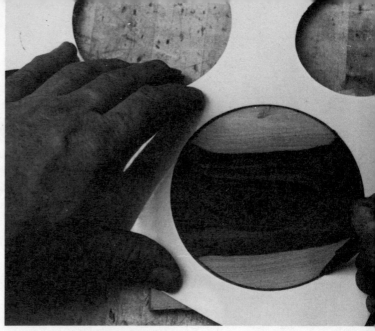

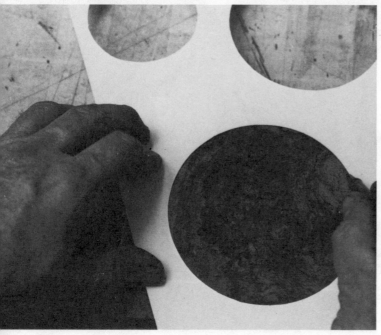

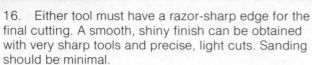

16.   Either tool must have a razor-sharp edge for the final cutting. A smooth, shiny finish can be obtained with very sharp tools and precise, light cuts. Sanding should be minimal.

17.   Select a piece of highly figured wood for the inlay.

A template with circles of various diameters is excellent for selecting the part of the wood you want to use. Make your own template from light cardboard or plastic sheet.

This is a piece of dark brown spalted myrtlewood.

18.   This is a piece of desert ironwood with sound sapwood and dark, golden-brown heartwood.

The template makes it easy to select the best part of the piece.

The inlay should be about 1/4'' larger in diameter than the recess in the top, to allow for gluing to a disc and cutting and fitting the inlay.

19.   Band saw the inlay to the desired size.

Glue the inlay directly to a wooden disc.

Paper may be used between the inlay and the disc, but the water in the glue sometimes will cause the thin inlay to warp and pull away from the disc, tearing the paper. I prefer to glue wood to wood. Later the inlay will be parted off with a parting tool.

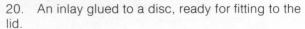

20.   An inlay glued to a disc, ready for fitting to the lid.

Note the beautiful figure in this piece of spalted myrtlewood.

21.   The wooden disc and inlay have been mounted to a screw-center faceplate.

Using a square-nose chisel, square the edge of the inlay.

22.   Check the lid against the inlay.

The inlay should have a slight taper, similar to the taper in the lid.

Remove small amounts of wood, and check frequently for proper fit.

23.   A correct fit is indicated when light pressure is needed to press the lid over the inlay.

Do not press too hard. The fragile edge of the recess in the top may break.

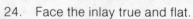

24.   Face the inlay true and flat.

A sharp square-nose is best for this job.

25.   Check the inlay with the same straightedge used to check the recess in the top.

26.   Check the final fit, and make any fine cuts needed to complete the fitting of the inlay to the top.

27.   As a final check, I put a bead of glue across the recess in the top piece.

28.   Place the top piece over the inlay, and rotate the top against the inlay.

This picture shows poor glue distribution. The only direct contact between the top and the inlay was at the edge of the recess.

Make a light cut on the inlay to solve the problem.

29.   This photo shows good distribution of glue.

The inlay and recess will make a tight fit.

30.   Place more glue in the recess, place the top over the inlay, and rotate the top until the glue beads out all around the edge of the inlay.

Clamp the two pieces together.

The lathe can be used as a clamp, or the pieces may be clamped together with other kinds of clamps.

31. True up the lip of the base of the box with a sharp square-nose tool.

Remove wood until the lip is 3/16″ to 1/8″ thick.

Cuts must be clean and true. The lip should require little or no sanding.

The lip needs to be shaped to provide contact with the lid at the top of the lip, with a little clearance at the shoulder of the lip. Various ways of doing this are shown in the next figure.

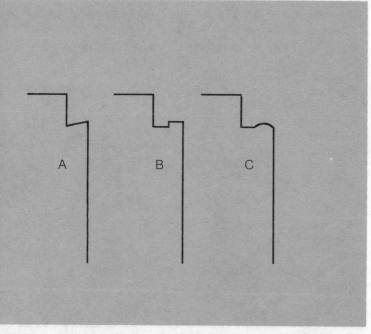

32. Any of these choices will make a very good fit, if the lid is fitted properly.

33. I prefer method A, because it is simple and easy to do.

Use a parting tool to bevel the lip and provide clearance as shown in A.

The clearance should be less than 1/64″. Just a little is all that is needed.

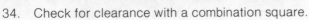

34.   Check for clearance with a combination square.

If necessary, make another light cut to obtain the clearance.

35.   Sand the lip very lightly. Use a rigid piece of abrasive paper, usually 150 grit.

36.   Measure the outside diameter of the lip.

This one measures about 2 ⅞″.

37.   Place the top piece on the lathe, and transfer the measurement of the lip diameter, less 1/8″ to 3/16″, to the inside of the top.

The shorter measurement gives plenty of allowance for error in cutting, at the same time giving a point at which to start checking the base lip with the lid.

38. Start the lathe. Use a pencil to transfer the point around the inside of the top.

39. Make a light cut across the inside of the top.

A sharp square-nose is best for the cut.

40. Check the fit of the lid with the base piece.

Continue enlarging the recess until the base piece makes a tight fit into the shallow recess.

Take light cuts and check frequently. There is little room for error at this point, and carelessness may ruin the lid.

41. When the lid fits the base, the recess needs to be made deep enough to accommodate the lip on the base piece.

Deepen the recess, but allow the recess to be beveled inward slightly to allow for final fitting of the lid to the base.

Be careful!

Take fine, light cuts with a sharp tool. The interior of the lid should not require sanding.

Flat-bottom lids should be straight and flat.

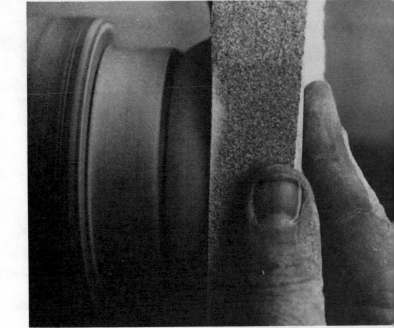

42. Use a flat block and abrasive paper to true up and smooth the rim of the lid.

43. Check the fit of the lid to the base piece.

Take light cuts, and check the fit after each cut.

The lid must fit tight, because the friction fit is all that will hold the top in place for the final turning.

44. The lid and base, showing the final fit. A good fit is indicated by a slight vacuum-produced "pop" when the lid is removed.

Note the way the figure matches in the pieces.

45. If necessary, lightly sand the interior of the lid, but *do not sand the inside lip* of the lid.

46. Using a parting tool, part the lid from the wooden disc.

Make the parting cut in the waste stock.

47. Fit the lid to the base, and finish turning the outside of the box to its final shape.

Use a sharp roundnose or gouge.

48. When the body of the box has been shaped, complete the turning of the top.

Take light cuts with a sharp tool.

Work carefully. The lid is held in place by the fit of the pieces, and jamming a tool will probably make the lid fly off and break.

49. Freshly sharpen the tool, and make final finishing cuts.

The final cuts should require very little sanding, usually starting with 150 or 220 grit paper.

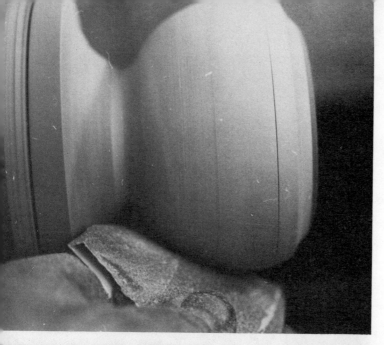

50.   Sand the box to its final finish, usually ending with 220 or 320 grit paper.

When sanding the lid, move the paper from the lid toward the bottom of the box. This will keep the lid in place. Otherwise the pressure from the sanding may make the lid come off.

51.   Separate the box from the wooden disc.

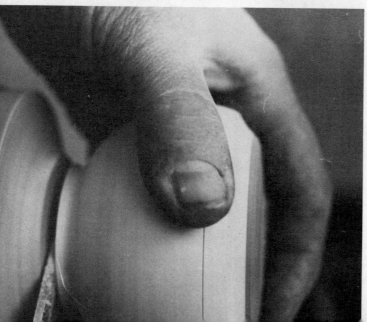

52.   Let the box rotate in your hand as the cut reaches the point of separation.

Continue with the parting cut, and keep the box in your hand.

53.   Place the base of the box on the step-tapered circular chuck.

Check for proper fit. One of the steps should fit the box, holding it in place with firm pressure.

(Construction of a circular chuck is shown in this book under "Tools and Jigs.")

54.   Masking tape can be used to further secure the box to the chuck. This is optional, because the fingers of the chuck should have been compressed enough to hold the box in place without the tape.

55.   Turn the foot on the box.

Use light cuts and a sharp tool.

158

56.   If necessary, make final cuts to clean up and give final shape to the foot.

A sharp skew and a shearing cut are being used to round the outside of the foot on the box.

57.   Complete the sanding.

58.   The finished box—lid in place, foot turned, and ready for finishing.

Top. Australian walnut. Stephen Hogbin.
Bottom. Black cherry. Stephen Hogbin.

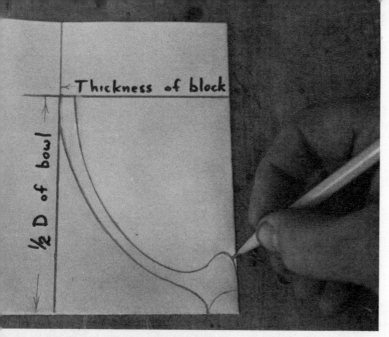

Segmented Forms

Segmented forms are those that have been turned, cut apart, and reassembled. This type of turning has been developed to an advanced state by Stephen Hogbin of North Bay, Ontario, Canada.

Other examples of Hogbin's work can be found in his book *Woodturning* (New York: Van Nostrand Reinhold, 1980).

The basic thrust of these turnings is that the shape of the cross section of the turning is often more interesting than the original turned form. Cutting and reassembling it in various ways gives it a personality and form of its own. Many of the smaller forms take on a natural form, reminding one of shells, cones, and other of nature's designs.

The following pictures show one way to approach these forms. This is only the beginning of possibilities for the craftsman. I hope new vistas will appear as one continues to experiment with this exciting idea and its numerous possibilities.

1.   Select a block of wood for the turning, and determine the basic dimensions of the completed turning.

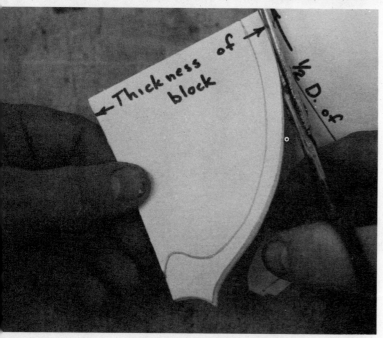

Fold a piece of paper into quarters, and lay out the shape of the section. This will represent one quarter of the turning, showing the appearance of the top view after the original turning has been cut apart and reassembled.

Usually the reassembled turning is oval shaped, the width being equal to twice the thickness of the block, and the length being equal to the diameter of the original turned piece.

2.   Using the valentine method, cut out the exterior shape and part of the interior shape on the paper drawing.

3.   Leave the center part; otherwise, the pattern will be flimsy and difficult to handle.

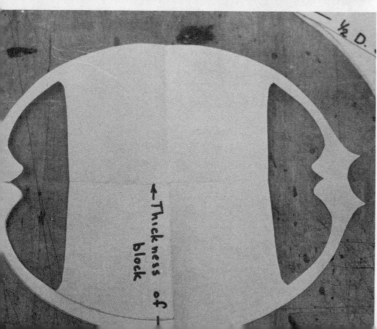

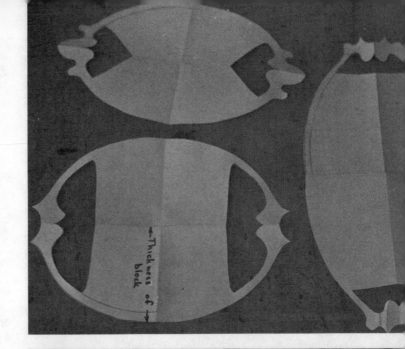

4. If you are not pleased with the results, make the necessary changes and try again. In fact, try several different shapes and select the one you like best.

Keep the patterns for future use.

5. Joint the block flat and true.

Lay out a circle, and cut out the block on a band saw.

Deeply indent the center point of the bottom of the turning block.

6. Cut out an extension block from a piece of softwood. The block needs to be for a small faceplate, with a thickness of 1½'' to 2''.

The extension block should be thick, because part of it will be removed during the turning process, and it must be thick enough to hold the screws as well as allowing part of it to be turned away when the base of turning is being shaped.

Drive a small finish nail into the center of the block, then cut it off, leaving 1/8'' or less exposed.

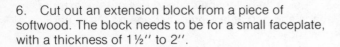
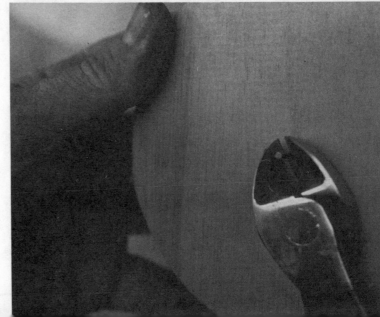

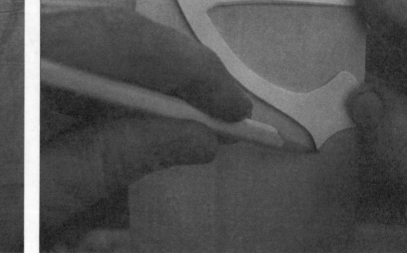

7.   Glue the extension block to the base of the turning block.

The finish nail should enter the center hole in the turning block.

The nail will hold the block in position while it is being clamped.

8.   Securely fasten the extension block to the face plate. The screws should not go deeper than 3/4'' into the extension block; otherwise, you may hit them with the turning tools.

9.   True up the edge of the block, using a sharp gouge or roundnose.

10.   Lay the pattern on the block, and mark the necessary points.

At this time visualize what the interior of the turning will look like. The pattern represents a cross-section of the actual turning.

11. A sharp gouge or roundnose can be used to cut the shape of the edge. Follow the shape of the pattern as nearly as you can. Any deviation from the pattern shape will be doubled when the form is cut apart and reassembled.

12. The profiles must be cut clean and sharp. Transition points must be definite and clear. If they are not, the turning will lose much of its crisp, sharp appearance.

13. Shape the outside of the turning. Use a gouge or roundnose. However, if the roundnose is used, make a final cleanup cut with a sharp gouge and a light shearing cut.

14. Shape the exterior of the turning down to the extension block. Be sure the curve of the surface can be extended without interruption to the center of the base. The curve should be pleasing to the eye and have good continuity. The pencil line on the turning shows the eventual shape of the base.

Keep in mind that this line will be the top outside edge of the form when it has been cut apart and reassembled.

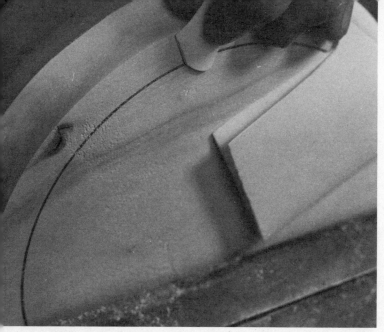

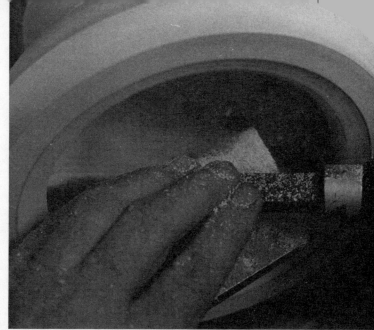

15.   Lay the pattern on the face of the turning and mark the transition points.

Note in your mind the final inside shape of the lip of the turning.

16.   Use a sharp roundnose to do the interior shaping of the piece.

17.   Using the straight roundnose, take light cuts, working as far back against the lip as you can.

Work carefully.

18.   The reverse curve inside the lip of the turning requires the use of a bent roundnose. This tool has been heated, bent on the flat plane, and resharpened for use.

Be careful. The pressure of the wood turning against the tool will twist the tool in your hand.

Take light cuts, and keep the tool sharp.

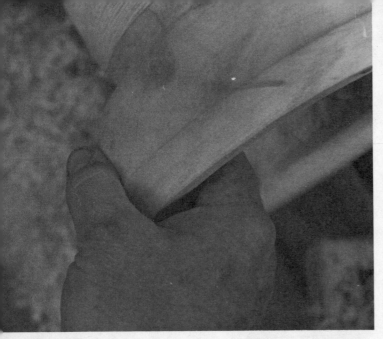

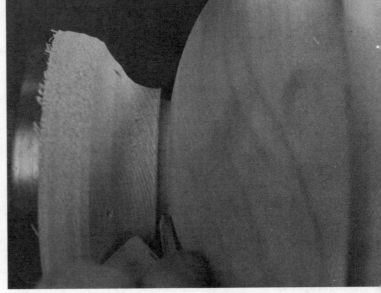

19.   Check for wall thickness frequently. The fingers make good calipers for rough thicknesses.

20.   The final wall thickness is critical to the appearance of the wall sections when the turning has been cut in two pieces. Any variation in thickness will show and cannot be changed once the turning has been cut.

Regular calipers will not work in places such as this, so I made a set of calipers that measure on the inside of the turning but can be read on the outside. They are crude but effective. The space indicated by the pencil point is the wall thickness at this area of the turning.

Uniform wall thickness, or gradual and controlled transition in thickness, is a must for a successful form of this type.

21.   When the interior of the turning has been completed, work on the exterior.

Carefully shape the exterior, working into the extension block to give room for the tools to be used.

Keep in mind that at the center of the turning the tool will be working mostly in the extension block, removing very little wood from the turning itself.

22.   The final shaping cut at the base is made with a sharp parting tool. This cut establishes the final shape of the base. The side of the parting tool rides against the turning, while the point is moved into the wood, shaping the base to final form.

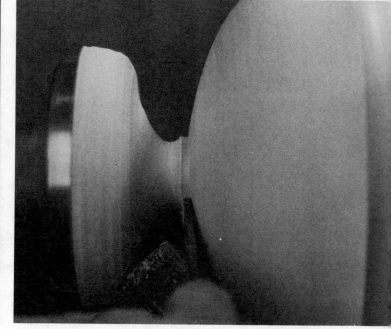

23.   Sand the bowl inside and out. The sequence of grits I use is usually 60, 80, 100, 150, 220, and 320.

24.   Sand the inside radius with folded paper, with steel wool supporting the curve of the paper.

Keep the curves smooth and clean.

25.   The point where curves meet must be kept sharp and crisp for good appearance.

26.   When the sanding has been completed, remove excess wood from the extension block with a roundnose.

Use the parting tool and continue separating the turning from the block.

Run the lathe at slow speed.

27. As the turning nears the point of separation, support it with a gloved hand, and complete the separation with the parting tool.

This requires a steady hand but is not difficult.

Allow the turning to spin freely in your hand, just using light pressure to support it. When it comes off, it is not difficult to hold. It is thin and light.

This works well on *small* turnings, not more than eight inches in diameter.

If you have reservations about doing this with the lathe running, stop the machine and saw the turning from the block. This will require a little more hand sanding but may make one feel more comfortable.

28. Use a sanding block and the usual sequence of papers to remove the remaining wood from the base.

When the sanding is complete, the area should show no flat spots or sanding marks.

Be patient and careful here. This point will be the top, outside edge of the form when it is completed.

29. The maximum diameter of the turning must be found. A good way to do this is with two try squares (as shown), measuring the distance between them.

The diameter of this piece reads 7 ⅝".

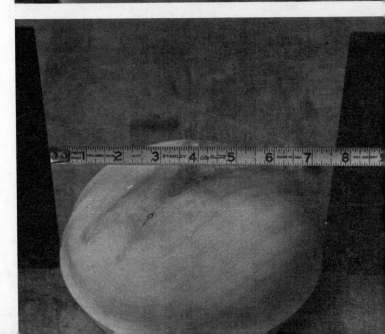

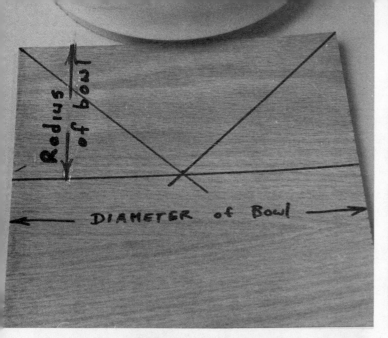

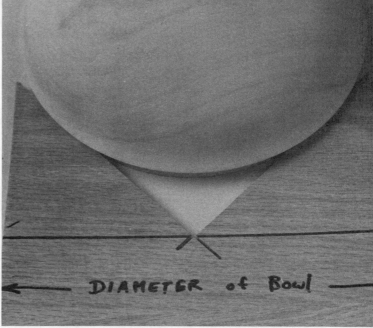

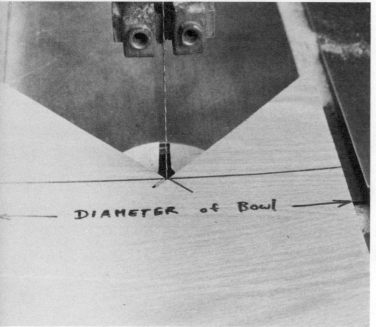

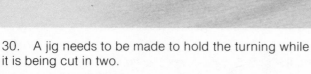

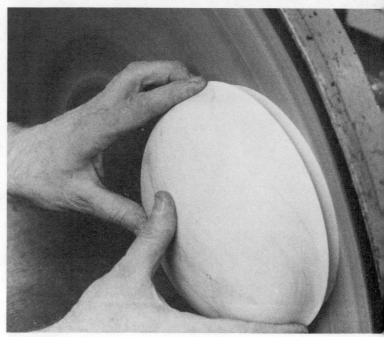

30. A jig needs to be made to hold the turning while it is being cut in two.

Cut a piece of 1/4'' plywood to a width equal to the diameter of the bowl.

Lay out the piece as shown.

31. Cut out the triangular piece. A band saw is ideal, but a hand saw would work equally well.

32. This jig is used to hold the turning in position while it is being cut in two on the band saw.

A carefully made jig will help ensure that the turning is cut into two equal pieces.

33. Before the piece is cut in two, lightly sand the top of the turning flat and true.

Do not remove more stock than is necessary to get the edge suitable for gluing.

If a disc sander is not available, lay a sheet of sandpaper on a flat surface such as a saw table, lay the turning top down, and move the turning back and forth across the sandpaper until the top is true and flat.

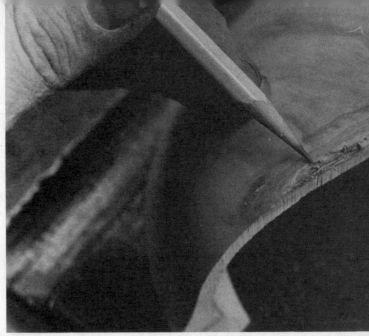

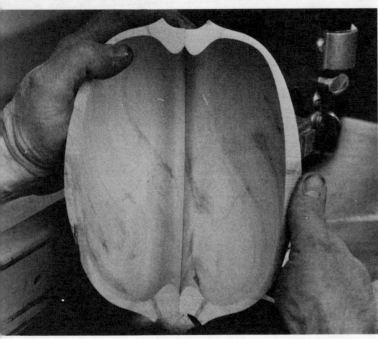

34. Using the jig and the band saw fence, cut the turning in two.

This could be done with a hand saw, but I would not advise using a table saw. There would be danger because of the blade height and the difficulty of controlling the pieces.

35. It is always exciting when one first reassembles the two pieces. At that time, it is simple to see that the final form is more interesting than the original turning.

36. If a piece is laid out and cut in two through a defect, the defect can be removed when the piece is sanded.

37. Before sanding the sawn edge, check the sanding table to be sure that it is square to the sanding disc.

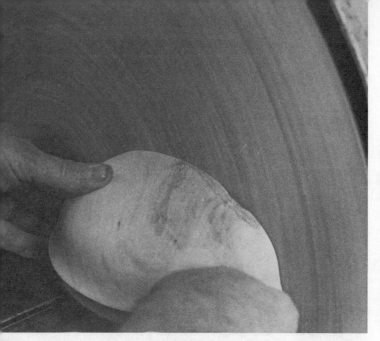

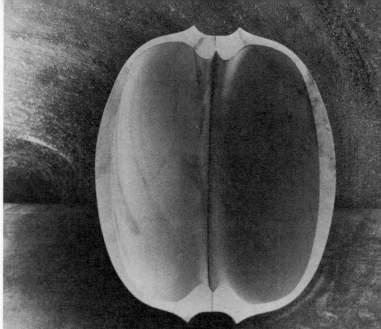

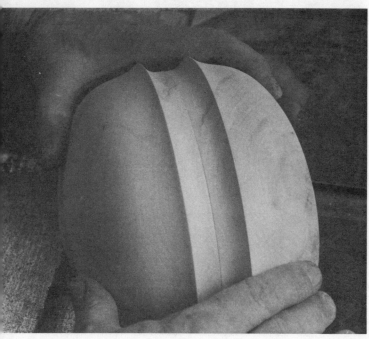

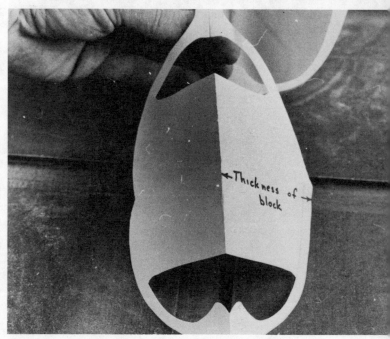

Thickness of block

38.   Sand the sawn edge of each piece.

Use light pressure, but hold the piece securely.

39.   Lay the sanded edges down on the table, and check the two pieces when they are placed together.

Continue sanding one piece or both until you are satisfied with the fit and appearance of the form.

40.   This piece has been sanded, fitted and glued up—a rather typical piece using the reassembly process, but quite pleasing and certainly more interesting than the original turning.

41.   A simple variation easily achieved is to remove more stock from one side of both halves, giving the form an asymmetrical appearance. The effect can be visualized by folding part of the pattern under. Try various form options, and select one that you want to produce.

42.   Using the sander, it is easy to remove unwanted material.

Sand each piece an equal amount, comparing the results frequently.

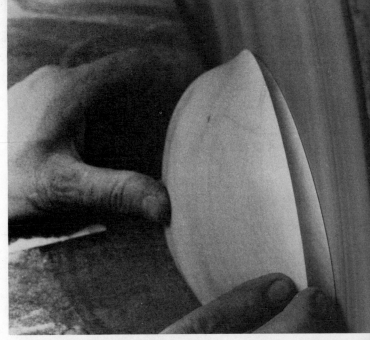

43.   The result of sanding about 5/8″ off each half of the turning.

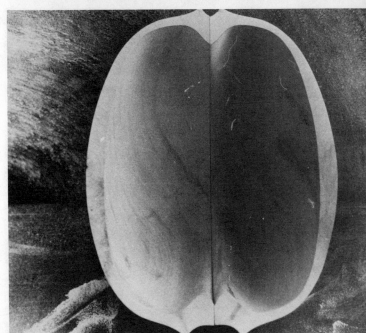

44.   Place a small amount of glue on each surface to be glued together. Using too much will make the squeeze out messy to remove.

Using your finger, spread a thin film on each surface to be glued.

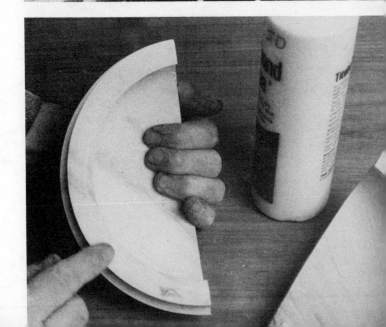

45.   These halves have been glued together using a rubbed joint. The pieces have been hand held for a few minutes, until the glue has set enough to hold them. For this type of gluing, a perfect fit is a necessity.

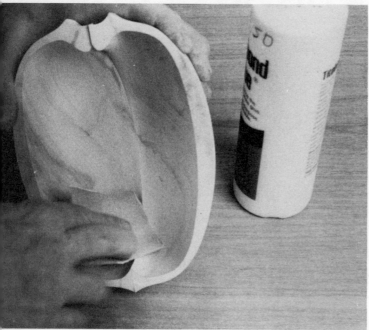

46.   With a sharp knife, remove the excess glue from the joints.

While the glue is still wet, sand the joined edges. They will practically disappear.

Let the piece set for a few hours.

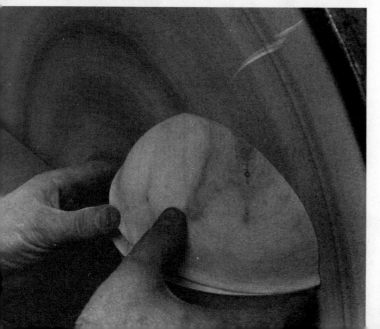

47.   A light cleanup sanding is usually needed to true up the top edge of the form.

48. The finished form.

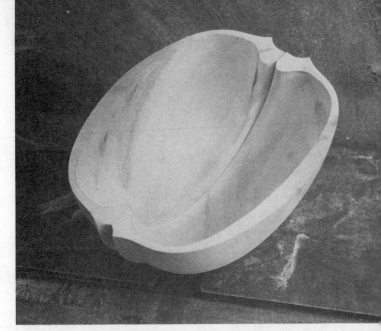

49. Giving the form a flat base can be done easily using the miter gauge and disc sander.

Clamp a flat board to the miter gauge as shown.

50. Holding the top of the form against the board, move the form against the sanding disc.

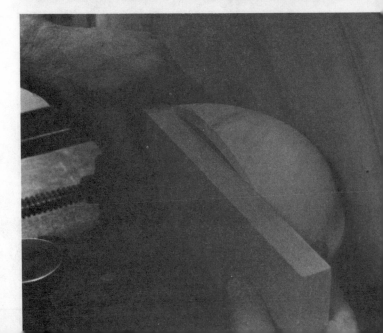

174

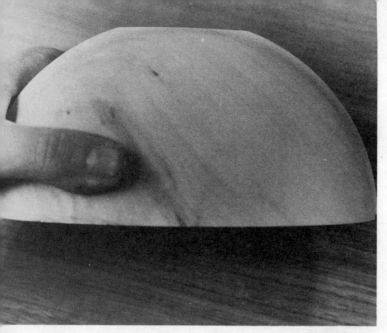

51.　Frequently check the base of the form.

Remove only enough material to give the form stability. Too much will give it a heavy appearance at the base, taking away from the excitement of the form.

52.　Note the interesting appearance of the base, as well as the even appearance of the parts.

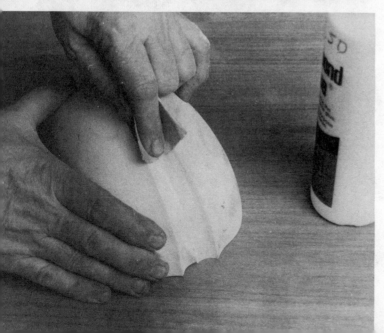

53.　Complete the final sanding, and get ready for finishing.

Assorted woods. Dale L. Nish.

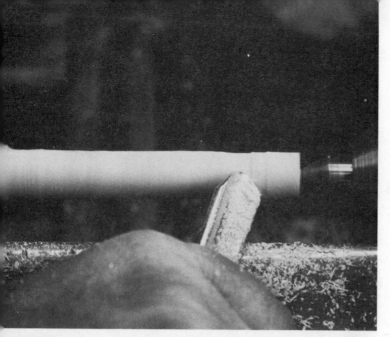

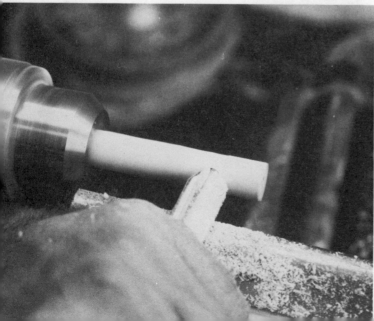

Miniatures

Miniature Goblets

Miniatures present an opportunity to turn a piece both challenging and intriguing. The delicate proportions seldom fail to amaze those who view them, at the same time impressing the viewer with the versatility and strength of wood as a material. Miniatures often contain sections that become translucent in a strong light, giving the appearance of a fragile shell or piece of bone. They have been in demand for many years; in fact, miniature turnings are a source of interest to antique collectors, and many pieces are more than a hundred years old.

The fragile sections in a miniature make dense, close-grained woods with straight grain the best choice for this type of turning. Lignum vitae sapwood, hard maple, cocobolo, and ebony are among woods with the required characteristics. Some turners prefer a white wood or the sapwood of a dark wood because they can follow the progress of the turning by examining the piece with a strong light, wall sections becoming translucent as the wall achieves the desired thickness.

Miniatures usually require the use of small tools, some no larger than a matchstick. I make miniature tools using concrete nails for the steel and dowel pieces for the handles. (Tool construction is discussed in detail under "Tools and Jigs.") Del Stubbs of Chico, California, is an excellent miniature turner.

1.   Use a piece of maple dowel, or turn a square piece of stock until it is round and 1/2" or less in diameter. The piece needs to be turned round and smooth so it can be fastened securely into a chuck. An alternative is to glue chuck the dowel into a wooden block fastened to the faceplate.

2.   This sequence shows a 1/2" capacity Jacobs chuck with the turning stock held securely in place.

Be sure the chuck is installed in a clean spindle. Give a sharp rap to set the chuck firmly in the spindle; the turning is done at high speed, and it is critical that the chuck not come loose. If it does, it might injure the operator, damage the equipment, or both.

3.   Start the lathe, and increase the speed until the gouge cuts clean and until there is no chatter or vibration in the stock. Usually I turn at about 2000 rpm for small pieces such as this, but the tools must be sharp and used properly. Increasing the lathe speed is not the whole solution to turning problems, but it might produce a cleaner cut if the tools are sharp and used properly.

I use a 1/2" gouge and a shearing cut to true up the stock.

4.   A shearing cut made with the skew turned over will make a clean cut and trim the end of the stock.

5.   Lay out the cup and base of the goblet, using the point of the skew to cut the layout lines.

Place the skew in a shearing position, and turn the outside of the cup. Use several light cuts.

6.   When the goblet cup is turned to the desired shape, sand lightly with 320 grit paper. In fact, a shearing cut may not require any sanding at all.

7. Lay the skew on its side, and open up the interior of the cup in successive cuts, working from the center to the outside.

Take light cuts, and keep the tool very sharp.

Do not penetrate past the bottom of the cup.

8. A miniature roundnose, very sharp and right from the stone, is used to complete the roughing out of the interior.

9. Using a sliver of wood as a gauge, check the cup for depth.

Remove stock until about 1/16″ of wood is left in the bottom of the cup.

10. Sharpen the roundnose, and with a finger lightly touching the cup, complete the turning.

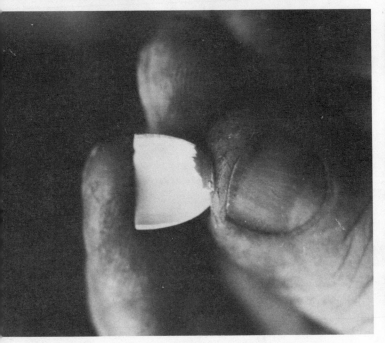

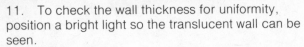

11.   To check the wall thickness for uniformity, position a bright light so the translucent wall can be seen.

This picture shows a cup that has been turned too thin in the bottom and is about to disintegrate, a crack appearing along the bottom and moving up to the rim. This piece is ruined, but it teaches a good lesson.

Use the light frequently. A wall of ideal thickness should show a dull glow from the rim to the bottom of the cup.

12.   This is the broken cup.

Note the variation in wall thickness. The top is still a little too thick and the bottom too thin.

Practice will solve the problem.

13.   Turning the skew over, turn the ring at the base of the cup. This step is optional, but it allows a little more stock to separate the cup from the stem.

14.   Use a small roundnose to shape the top of the stem and the base of the ring.

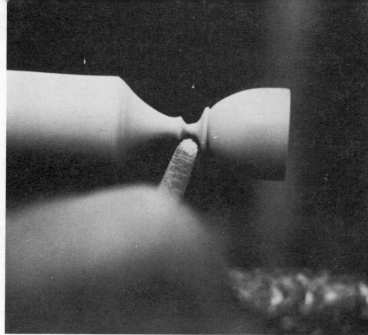

15.   Complete the turning of the ring.

16.   Using a gouge, rough out the stem and the base of the goblet.

The main secret of turning miniatures, or any thin sections for that matter, is *always work from thin sections toward the thick stock.*

Thin sections have little weight or mass, and working from the thin wood to the thick wood eliminates vibration, the major cause of failure in small or fragile turnings.

17.   Continue shaping the stem.

18.   Take light cuts. Use a sharp tool, and keep a steady hand. Good luck!

19. Lightly sand the stem with 320 grit paper, rolled in a pencillike shape. Be patient!

20. Using a parting tool, partially separate the base from the stock piece.

21. The shape of the base is optional, but strive for simplicity in detail and design.

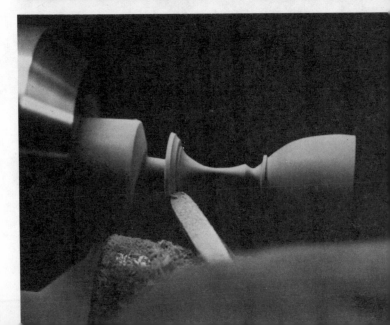

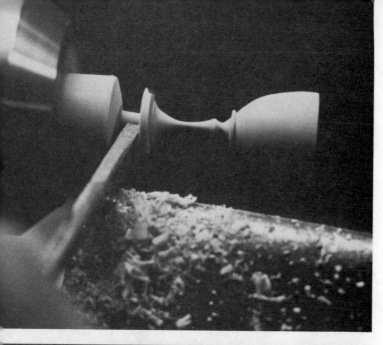

22.   Still using the parting tool, make a slightly concave cut into the base of the goblet.

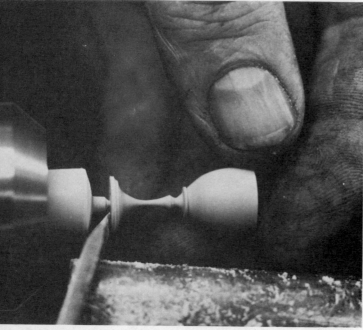

23.   Complete the concave cut with a small skew.

Catch the turning with your fingers as it separates from the stock piece.

24.   The miniature is complete, except for using a sharp knife to remove the small nub in the center of the goblet base.

Handle the turning with care. It will become someone's treasure!

Miniature Plates or Bowls

These small turnings are fun to do, and an exquisite piece is a source of delight to the person fortunate enough to acquire it. Because miniatures are very small, they can be turned from woods of unusual color and figure, received from distant lands or acquired locally. Hard, dense woods such as the ebonies, lignum vitae, cocobolo, and rosewood, or high-figured native woods such as crotch figure in ash, walnut, and cherry make excellent choices. Expensive woods become inexpensive when they are used for miniatures.

Miniature plates and bowls can be turned using similar procedures, the only difference being the change in dimension of the pieces.

1.   The band-sawed blank can be glued to the extension block, or mounted using double-faced tape as shown here.

2.   The double-faced tape is a quick and easy way to mount small pieces of stock, which exert little pressure when being turned.

Cut off enough tape to cover the area of the blank.

Cut the tape into pieces, if necessary. Fasten the tape to the block, and remove the cover paper.

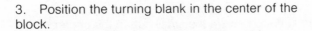

3.   Position the turning blank in the center of the block.

Mount the assembly on the headstock spindle, and move the tailstock into position.

Clamp the tailstock to the bed, and advance the tailstock spindle until firm pressure is exerted against the blank.

Leave the pressure on for a few minutes, to allow the tape to adhere to both surfaces.

4. Using a sharp gouge, true up the face of the blank.

5. True up the edge of the blank, and cut away part of the extension block (to simplify the process of shaping the outside of the bowl).

The "smoke" in the photo is caused by small ribbons of tape spinning off a very sharp roundnose tool.

6. Position the tool rest, and use a sharp roundnose to shape the interior of the bowl. For clean, smooth cuts, set the lathe at about 2000 rpm; the cutting circle is very small.

Take light accurate cuts. Do not force the tool.

7. Shape the interior of the bowl, leaving about 3/16'' of wood in the bottom. This is enough to allow a foot to be turned, leaving a final interior thickness of about 1/16'' to 3/32''.

8.   Shape the exterior of the bowl, leaving a final wall thickness of about 1/16''.

9.   Sand the inside and outside of the bowl, finishing up with 320 grit abrasive paper.

10.   Using firm, continuous pressure, gently separate the bowl from the block.

11.   True up the face of the extension block.

Use a gouge or roundnose chisel.

12. Drill a 3/8'' or larger hole through the center of the extension block.

If a drill chuck is not available, use a skew chisel to bore the hole.

This hole is necessary: Through it a pencil will push the finished piece out of the rabbet turned into the block.

13. Use the point of the skew to make a series of shallow cuts in the face of the block.

These will be used as guide lines for cutting the rabbet to hold the bowl.

14. Check the fit frequently, and cut the rabbet to a depth of about 3/16'' to 1/4''.

Press fit the bowl into the rabbet. A firm, secure fit is necessary for holding the bowl in position to complete the turning of the base.

If the rabbet gets too large and the fit is loose, face off the piece and turn a rabbet that fits the bowl correctly.

Insert the bowl, and seat it securely in the rabbet.

15. Using a small, sharp roundnose, turn the exterior to final shape.

Take light cuts. Do not take off too much wood; you might cut through the piece and ruin the bowl.

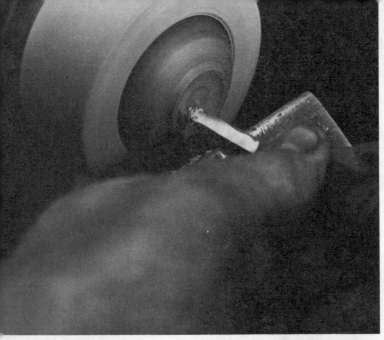

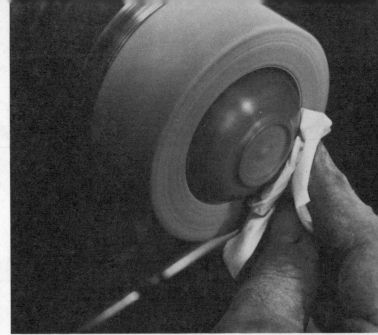

16.   A miniature roundnose is used for the final shaping of the inside of the foot.

17.   Sand the bowl, finishing with 320 grit paper.

18.   This bowl was turned from lignum vitae, so the final finish is a high-speed buffing with a soft flannel cloth or piece of soft tissue paper.

19.   Notice the soft sheen, and delicate shape of the base.

Miniature turnings are fun to do.

20.   Remove the faceplate from the lathe, and insert the eraser end of a pencil into the hole in the block.

Using a soft, tapping touch, gently force the bowl from the rabbet.

Easy does it. The wall thickness is 1/16″ or less.

When this piece was held up to the light, the light-colored areas were translucent.

Miniatures with Lids

Miniatures with lids add a little extra challenge to the turning and are treasured by the collector. And a lid or cover gives the piece another dimension—a certain mystique. Few people will pick up such a piece and not remove the lid. A certain inquisitiveness in most of us, both young and old, needs satisfying.

Recently I made a miniature lidded box that would hold only one jelly bean. I gave this box to my grandson, who carried his "jelly bean box" with him for several days and still had it when he returned to his home in Chicago. He would open it frequently, peer inside, replace the lid, and put the box back into his pocket. He was satisfied even though the jelly bean was gone. But he was happier yet to find one there. He would pop it into his mouth and then replenish his supply from the candy jar on the cupboard. Such is a little child—so are most adults.

Accept the challenge. Try a miniature with a lid.

1.   Stock for miniatures can be held with a Jacobs chuck or a three-jaw chuck or with the stock held by the glue-chuck method. Most of us do not possess the mechanical chucks, but the glue-chuck method is available to all.

Select a piece of stock a little larger than needed for the turning, and turn one end to a cylinder.

2.   Securely fasten a scrap disc about 1/4″ thick to the faceplate.

With a suitable bit, bore a hole in the disc. The hole should be a little less in diameter than the diameter of the turned cylinder.

3. Using a sharp skew, enlarge the hole until it makes a tight fit with the cylinder.

Do not allow a loose fit. It would be weak, and glue is not a filler.

4. Spread glue around the contact surfaces on both pieces.

Use the lathe tailstock as a clamping device, and force the cylinder into the hole. Allow it to set for twenty minutes or longer, then remove the assembly from the lathe and allow it to set overnight before continuing the turning.

5. Mark off the section needed for the lid. The length must include the total lid plus a little extra for waste and trim.

Reduce the diameter of the lid section until it is the correct size.

Using a skew chisel, clean up the surface with a shearing cut.

6. Shape the lid using a gouge and a shearing cut.

Keep in mind that the top of the lid is against the solid stock. The lid opening is at the end of the stock.

7.   If the lid has a convex shape on the top, use a skew chisel (as shown) to turn the top to size.

8.   A sharp gouge is a good tool for producing a concave surface on the top piece.

At this point, remove the stock until about 1/2" is left. This will allow one to see the general shape of the top but will leave enough stock to keep the lid from breaking off or chattering.

9.   Turn the skew over, and clean up the base of the lid with a light shearing cut.

10.   Rough out the interior of the lid with a skew chisel.

Start at the center and work out.

The final cut must be square to the base of the lid. One way to make the correct cut is to line up the skew chisel with the lathe bed. Keep the skew parallel to the lathe bed and make a light cut.

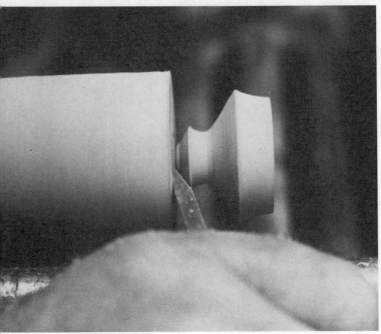
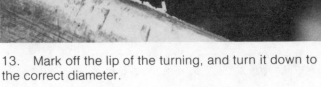

11. If the interior of the lid is to be flat, use a miniature square-nose chisel.

If the interior is to be rounded, use a sharp roundnose to make the cut.

Take light cuts with very sharp tools, as the inside is not sanded.

12. Part off the lid with a skew chisel.

Do not let the lid drop; it may break.

13. Mark off the lip of the turning, and turn it down to the correct diameter.

Check frequently.

I like to taper the lip away from the shoulder, continuing until the lid will just fit on the edge of the lip.

14. A snug press fit is a must, as the lid must be held in place for the completion of the top of the lid.

15. If the lid happens to fit too loosely, turn another lip just a little larger than the first one.

Use the original lip as a guide to the approximate size, then part it off.

16. With the lid in place, rough turn the bowl of the turning to diameter.

Mark the base of the bowl with a parting tool.

17. Turn the convex side of the bowl with a skew, making a shearing cut.

18. Shape the concave area of the bowl with a sharp gouge, making a shearing cut.

19. A strip of masking tape holding the top to the bowl is good insurance while the top is being completed.

It may not be necessary, but the one who is turning will usually feel more secure and confident.

20. A gouge is used to shape the top.

21. A skew is used to shape the finial.

22. A sharp skew can be used for delicate shaping.

23. It will also do an excellent job on delicate trimming and cutting.

24. Sand the outside of the top with 320 grit paper.

25. Remove the masking tape, and sand the rest of the bowl and lid.

Fold the sandpaper to a shape that will fit the bowl.

Light finger pressure on the lid will prevent the the lid from spinning off during sanding.

26. Rough out the inside of the bowl with a skew, working from the center to the outside. Take light cuts, and be careful not to go too deep.

27.   Complete the inside of the bowl with a square-nose or roundnose chisel, depending on the shape of the inside bottom.

The tools must be very sharp: The inside will not be sanded.

Note the wall thickness as compared with the end of a ball-point pen.

28.   Rough shape the base and stem with a gouge.

29.   Complete the shaping of the base of the bowl.

30.   Using a small skew chisel, make a small, flat ring at the base of the bowl.

31. Complete the stem and base with a small gouge and a fine shearing cut.

32. Remove stock from the base to allow for the finish turning.

33. Using the skew, make a V-cut to partially separate the base from the stock.

34. Trim the base with a sharp skew chisel.

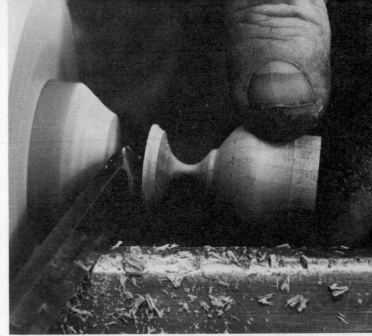

35. A sharp miniature roundnose is used to complete the design of the base.

36. Using a parting tool, partially separate the base from the stock.

Make a concave underside on the base.

Note the slight angle of the parting tool.

37. Complete the parting off with the skew chisel.

38. The turned miniature, top in place ready for the finishing to be completed.

Miniatures with Loose-Fitting Lids

Many opportunities exist for the turner of covered containers. Some excellent examples are tea bowls from the Orient, loose-lidded early American sugar bowls, and various Scandinavian pieces. Nor is it essential to turn miniatures representing actual pieces. However, it may add to the piece to be able to identify it as a specific type.

Members of my family have lived in Japan for several years, and the Japanese culture has influenced all of us. I, for one, am captivated by the design of Oriental ceramics, and particularly by Japanese art pieces. The following sequence illustrates the procedure for turning a miniature Japanese tea bowl.

Turners who read this sequence should be able to adapt techniques from similar problems in earlier sequences. It is not anticipated that readers would make tea bowls only. The following procedure can be used for many different pieces, miniatures and larger.

1. Select a piece of stock large enough to make both pieces of the turning. If the stock must be glued up, place the glue line where it will be removed when the two parts are separated.

Turning both pieces from the same piece of stock eliminates the need to glue up two pieces to two scrap blocks and fasten the assembly to two faceplates.

2. Using a lathe speed of 1200–1800 rpm and a sharp gouge or roundnose, turn the stock into a smooth cylinder.

Reduce the diameter of the stock to the rough diameter of the lid.

In this sequence the lid is smaller than the bowl.

3. Rough shape the lid, then make a cut with the parting tool, establishing the point between the lid and the base of the bowl.

4. The final shaping of the lid is accomplished with a very sharp, small roundnose chisel.

Light cuts and a sharp tool mean a smooth surface requiring very little sanding.

5. The inside top of the lid is being shaped with a miniature roundnose.

6. Sand lightly, ending with 320 grit sandpaper.

7. Part off the lid from the stock. Do not drop the lid; the outside of it is finished.

8. Turn a hole into the stock, a hole that will give a tight press fit to the top of the lid.

The depth of the hole is a little less than the shoulder height of the lid, because the part entering the hole should rest on the bottom to allow the piece to center and turn true.

9. Press fit the lid into the hole. Move the tailstock into position to give another point of pressure and additional support while roughing out the inside of the lid.

10. Rough out the inside of the lid using a small roundnose.

Leave a small post in the center where the tailstock center is holding the lid in place.

11. When most of the roughing out has been completed, move the tailstock out of the way and complete the turning of the lid.

Sand the inside until you are satisfied with the finished surface.

Remove the lid from the assembly, and set it aside until it is needed.

12. Partially separate the bottom of the bowl from the scrap stock.

The parting tool is cutting into the finished part because this cut is the beginning of the base.

13. Turn out the inside of the base piece.

Check frequently to be sure of a good fit.

A lid that fits well sits in the opening without sideways movement but can be removed with little force.

Making the interior too large will ruin the piece.

14. Leave a small shoulder to support the lid, then complete turning the inside of the lid.

15. A sharp roundnose is used to shape the outside of the bowl.

16. Leave a finished wall thickness of about 1/16''.

Sand the outside of the bowl before parting the piece off the scrap block.

17.   Using a sharp parting tool, separate the bowl from the scrap block.

18.   True up the face of the scrap block, and turn a recess into the block.

The recess must fit the outside diameter of the bowl so as to allow the bowl to be press fitted into the recess.

Bore a hole through the center of the block (see Figure 12 under "Miniature Plates or Bowls").

An extra precaution is to tape the bowl to the block. Otherwise, a tool may catch the bowl and pull it out of the recess.

19.   Shape the inside and outside of the foot, and blend the shape of the bowl into the base.

A sharp, miniature roundnose works well for this operation.

20.   Complete the sanding of the bowl, using the usual series of abrasive papers.

21.   The finished miniature Japanese tea bowl.

This bowl was made from Andaman padauk, a red, naturally oily wood. It was chosen because many such bowls were lacquered in bright colors.

Gallery of Craftsmen

Walnut. 8'' maximum dimension. Stephen Hogbin.

Above. Bowl, 7″ diameter. Soft maple. Stephen Hogbin.

Below. Bowl, 8″ diameter. Black cherry. Stephen Hogbin.

Above. Bowl, 8″ diameter. Black cherry, Stephen Hogbin.

Below. Bowl, 6½″ diameter. English walnut. Dale L. Nish.

Above. Clock face. Ebony and ivory. Frank E. Cummings, III. Cummings's description: ''Each of the fourteen gears was made by hand. The outer rims are of black African wood. The inner support systems are made of ivory and are capped with matching star sapphires with 18-carat gold bezels. There are three springs in the clock, and they also are made of ivory.''

Facing page. Clock. Frank E. Cummings, III. Standing 68'' high, the clock has a case of ebony and ivory.

Above. Lamp. Black cherry. Don Kelly. *Photo by Rosemary Carroll.*

Facing page top. Landscape plate, 1″ X 13″. Assorted woods. William Patrick.

Facing page bottom. Bowl. Spalted maple. William Patrick.

Above. Lamp, 16″ X 10½″. Black walnut—segmented ring construction with top and bottom full pie-shaped segments. Bob White. *Photo by Rick Sniffin.*

Facing page. Lamp. Black cherry. Don Kelly. *Photo by Rosemary Carroll.*

Top. Bowl, 2½″ X 4¾″. Desert ironwood. Bruce Mitchell.

Bottom. Bowl, 3¼″ X 8″. Honduras rosewood. Bruce Mitchell.

Calendar jar, 8½″ X 12″. Assorted woods, stave
construction with inlaid designs. Giles Gilson. *Photo
by Rick Siciliano.*

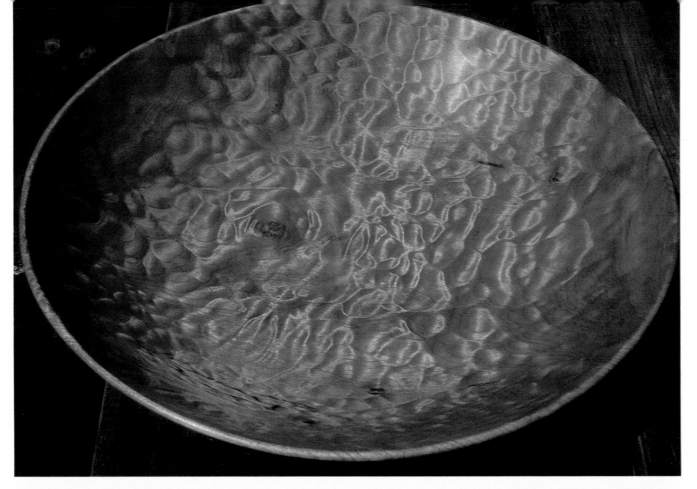

Top. Bowl, 3½″ X 16″. Quilted maple. Al Stirt.
Bottom. Bowl, 3½″ X 6″. White pine burl. Al Stirt.

Natural top bowl, 5″ X 10″. Maple burl. Mark
Lindquist. *Photo by Robert Aude.*

Above. Bowl, 6″ X 11″. Spalted yellow birch. Mark Lindquist. *Photo by Robert Aude.*

Below left. Vase, 6″ X 2½″. Spalted maple. Melvin Lindquist. *Photo by Robert Aude.*
Below right. Vase, 10″ X 4½″. Spalted maple. Melvin Lindquist. *Photo by Robert Aude.*

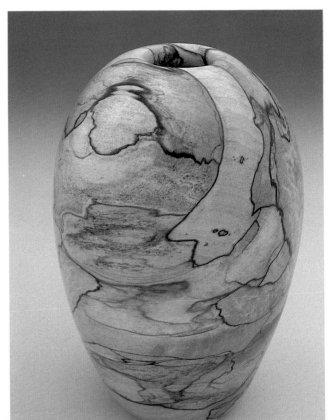

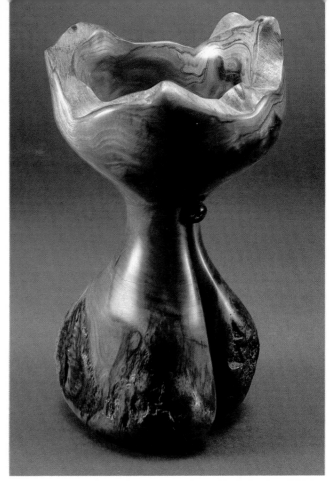

Above left. Natural top bowl, 10″ X 6″. Manzanita burl. Melvin Lindquist. *Photo by Robert Aude.*

Above right. Vase. Elm burl. Mark Lindquist. *Photo by Robert Aude.*

Below. Bowl, 5″ X 10″. Maple Burl. Melvin Lindquist. *Photo by Robert Aude.*

Facing page. Hollow turning, 9¼″ X 8″. Desert ironwood. David Ellsworth.

Top. Hollow turning, 5″ X 11″. Figured walnut. David Ellsworth.

Bottom. Hollow turning, 4″ X 11″. Walnut root. David Ellsworth.

Top. Bowls, (large) 1½″ X 12″ and (small) 2½″ X 5½″. Wormy ash. Dale L. Nish.

Bottom left. Bowl, 5½″ X 13″. Wormy ash. Dale L. Nish.

Bottom right. Plate, 1½″ X 17″. Sycamore. Dale L. Nish.

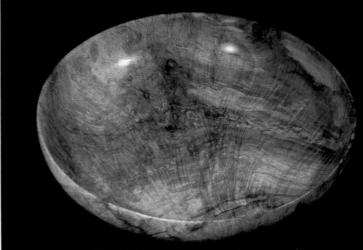

Top. Bowl, 6½'' X 13½''. Grafted walnut (English and claro). Dale L. Nish.
Bottom left. Plate, 1½'' X 12''. Oak burl. Dale L. Nish.
Bottom right. Bowl, 2½'' X 13''. Spalted silver maple. Dale L. Nish.

Facing page. Bowl, 27″ diameter. Figured tulipwood. Ed Moulthrop.

Above. Bowl, 33″ diameter. Figured tulipwood. Ed Moulthrop.

Right. Bowl, 9″ diameter. Figured tulipwood. Ed Moulthrop.

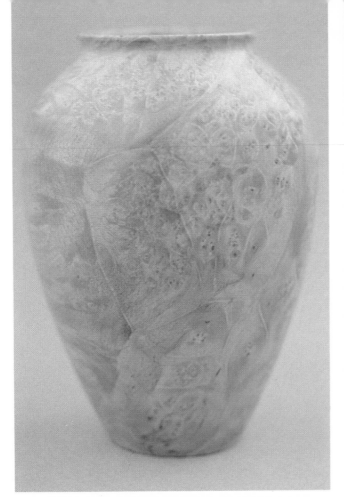
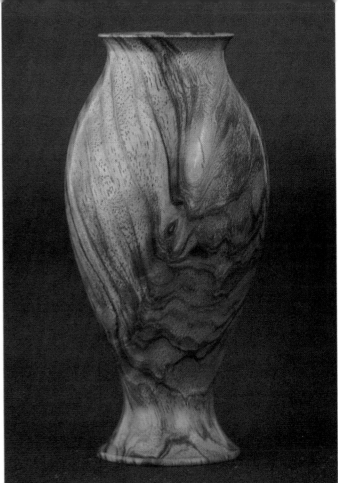

Top left. Vase. Lilac. Del Stubbs.
Top right. Vase. Black walnut. Del Stubbs.
Bottom. Covered box, 1¼″ X 3″. English walnut. Del Stubbs.

Top left. Bowl, 6½″ X 6½″. Bay laurel burl. Bruce Mitchell.

Top right. Bowl, 5¾″ X 10″. Fiddleback eucalyptus. Bruce Mitchell.

Bottom left. Bowl, 4½″ X 13″. Spalted red alder. Bruce Mitchell.

Bottom right. Bowl, 5¾″ X 9½″. Black walnut. Bruce Mitchell.

Top left. Bowl, 2½″ X 6″. Rotted crotch cottonwood. John Secor.

Top right. Bowl, 3″ X 7″. Spalted chestnut. Don Porter.

Bottom left. Hollow turning, 3½″ X 5″. Cottonwood. Kip Christensen.

Bottom right. Compote, 10″ X 8½″. Claro walnut. Byrd Pearson.

Facing page top. Covered bowl, 8½″ X 10″. Claro walnut. E. N. Pearson.

Facing page bottom. Covered bowl, 10″ X 11½″. Claro walnut. E. N. Pearson.

Facing page top. Bowl, 2½″ X 10″. Claro walnut, turned and then hand carved. Max Weaver.

Facing page bottom. Compote, 9″ X 7″. Cherry. Edwin C. Hinckley.

Top. Bowl, 5″ X 9½″. Figured bay laurel. Bruce Mitchell.

Bottom Bowl, 2½″ X 5¾″. Bay laurel burl. Bruce Mitchell.

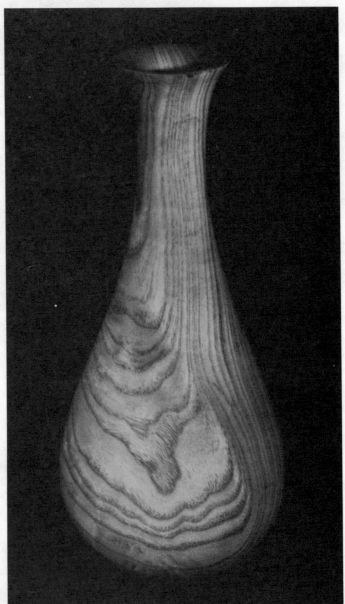

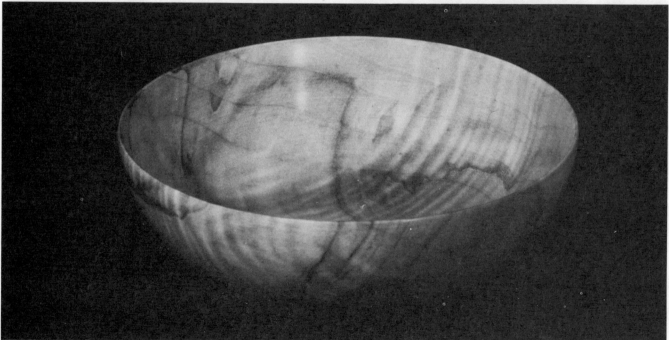

Facing page, top left. Vase, 6″ X 2½″. English walnut. Randall Nish.

Facing page, top right. Vase, 6¾″ X 2¾″. Ash. Randall Nish.

Facing page bottom. Bowl, 2½″ X 6″. Black walnut. Randall Nish.

Top. Bowl, 2¼″ X 6¾″. Black walnut. Brian Nish.
Bottom. Bowl, 2″ X 5″. Silver maple. Brian Nish.

Above. Clock. Leo Doyle.
Below. Container. Leo Doyle.
Facing page. Clock. Leo Doyle.

Above. Cake tray, 5¾″ X 9″. Claro walnut. Byrd Pearson.

Facing page top. Bowl, 4″ X 22″. Mahogany. Rude Osolnik.

Facing page bottom. Bowl, 5½″ X 11″. Stacked veneers. Rude Osolnik.

Above. Lotus bowl, 30″ diameter. Tulipwood. Ed Moulthrop.

Facing page top. Bowl, 22″ diameter. Figured tulipwood. Ed Moulthrop.

Facing page bottom. Bowl, 20″ diameter. Figured tulipwood. Ed Moulthrop.

Above. Bowl, 3½″ X 5″. Maple burl. Al Stirt. *Photo by Robert E. Barrett.*

Below. Bowl, 4″ X 9¼″. Butternut, with hand-carved exterior surface. Al Stirt. *Photo by Robert E. Barrett.*

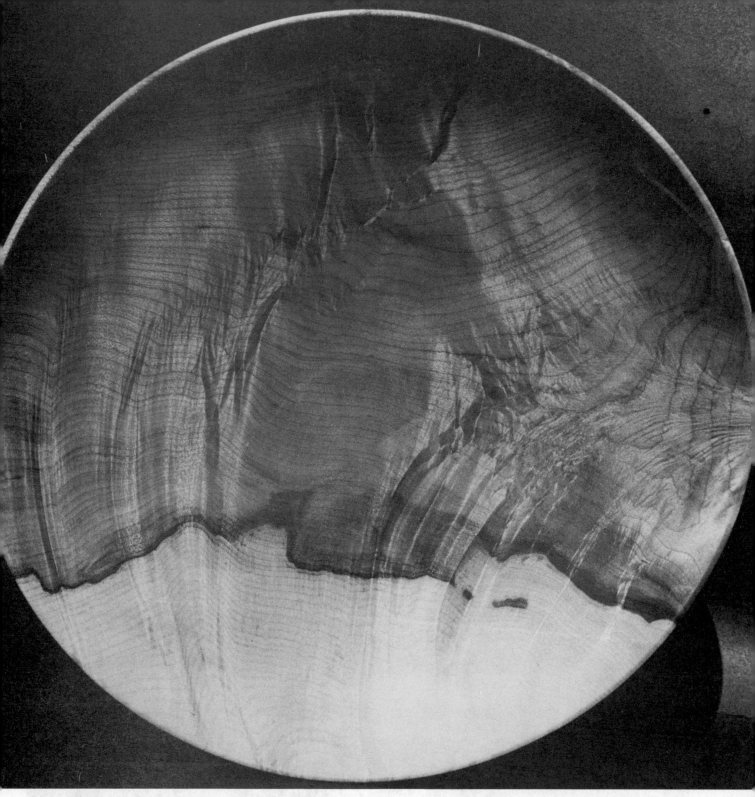

Plate, 2½″ X 13″. Sugar maple crotch. Al Stirt. *Photo by Roy Gifford.*

Below. Weed pots, largest piece, 5" X 3". Mesquite with sapwood perforated by powder-post beetles. Dale L. Nish.

Above. Weed pots: diameter, 4½"; height, 5½". Apricot with natural surfaces. Dale L. Nish.

Facing page. Weed pot, 5¾" X 4". Indian rosewood. Dale L. Nish.

Above. Bowl, 2¾'' X 5¾''. Mistletoe walnut. Dale L. Nish.

Below. Bowl, 5'' X 8''. Black walnut. Dale L. Nish.

Above. Hollow turning, 3½" X 5¼". Maple. Kip Christensen.

Below. Hollow turning, 3" X 6". Pear. Kip Christensen.

Top. Bowl, 2½″ X 8″. Wenge. Merle McKinnon.
Bottom. Bowl, 2½″ X 13″. Indian laurel. Max E. McKinnon.

248

Top. Covered bowl, 6½″ X 11¾″. Silver maple. Dale L. Nish.

Bottom. Bowl, 2¾″ X 5″. Black acacia. Dale L. Nish.

249

Above. Bowl, 9″ X 19″. English walnut with natural defects. Dale L. Nish.

Below. Bowl, 5½″ X 13″. Grafted walnut (English and black). Dale L. Nish.

Above. Bowl, 5½'' X 8½''. Black walnut with lip
shaped after turning. Dale L. Nish.

Below. Bowl, 3¼'' X 5''. Spalted myrtlewood. Dale L.
Nish.

Above. Plate, 1½″ X 10½″. Ash attacked by beetles and borers. Dale L. Nish.

Below. Bowl, 2½″ X 7″. Ash attacked by beetles and borers. Dale L. Nish.

Index

About the Author

Dale L. Nish, author of the immensely successful *Creative Woodturning,* is a totally involved woodworker/teacher whose professional interests overlap completely his avocation. Continually in search of new methods and procedures, he has visited design centers, wood-manufacturing operations, and craft shops worldwide. He is in constant demand as a workshop leader and has been a visiting professor at Washington State University. His students are continually impressed with his ease and speed in turning a rough chunk of wood into a work of art.